What's
Baptism
All About?

Herbert Mjorud

CREATION HOUSE
CAROL STREAM, ILLINOIS

Published by Creation House, 499 Gundersen Drive,
Carol Stream, Illinois 60187
Distributed in Canada: Beacon Distributing Ltd.,
104 Consumers Drive, Whitby, Ontario L1N 5T3
Distributed in Australia: Oracle Australia, Ltd.,
18-26 Canterbury Road, Heathmont, Victoria 3135

Scripture quotations marked RSV are from the Revised
Standard Version of the Bible, copyrighted 1946, 1952,
© 1971, 1973 by the Division of Christian Education of the
National Council of the Churches of Christ in the U.S.A., and
used by permission.

ISBN 0-88419-173-7

Library of Congress Catalog Card No. 77-80413

Printed in the United States of America

Contents

Introduction:

Divisiveness over an elementary doctrine

"Go therefore and make disciples of all nations, baptizing them *in the name of the Father and of the Son and of the Holy Spirit, teaching them to observe all that I have commanded you; and lo, I am with you always, to the close of the age" (Matthew 28:19,20 RSV).*

"He who believes and is baptized *will be saved; but he who does not believe will be condemned" (Mark 16:16 RSV).*

"And Peter said to them, 'Repent, and be baptized *every one of you in the name of Jesus Christ for the forgiveness of your sins' " (Acts 2:38 RSV).*

"There is one body and one Spirit, just as you were called to one hope that belongs to your call, one Lord, one faith, one baptism, *one God and Father of us all, who is above all and through all and in all" (Ephesians 4:4-6 RSV).*

"Therefore leave the doctrine of the first principles of Christ, let us go on unto perfection; not laying again the foundation of repentance from dead works, and of faith toward God, of the doctrine of baptisms, *and of laying on of hands, and of resurrection of the dead, and of eternal judgment" (Hebrews 6:1,2).*

Jesus Christ, the founder and Lord of the Kingdom of God, has commanded his followers to "go into all the world and make disciples of all nations, baptizing them." He said that they who believe and are baptized shall be saved, but those who do not believe shall be condemned. He did not say to make disciples by baptizing, but to make disciples and baptize them. A disciple is a believer and baptism is for such a person.

The true church has been baptizing now for some two thousand years; however, there have been different interpretations and some abuses and misuses of baptism. These different interpretations have been divisive, causing splits and schisms in the body of Christ. Each denomination teaches its own dogma on baptism as explicit truth, to be accepted without question. Each can show from the Scriptures how its own interpretation is the correct doctrine and, therefore, must be adhered to by its followers. These differences of opinion have kept groups isolated from each other.

In these days of ecumenical efforts in evangelism and other attempts at unity, people have simply understood that baptism must be left out of public proclamation of the message. It is too controversial.

Billy Graham, for example, does not speak on this subject in his large ecumenical meetings. While in Seattle, Washington, some years ago for a city-wide crusade, he was badgered by many pastors into speaking on the subject. He did, expressing the typical Baptist teaching, for he was, and still is, in the Baptist tradition. His sermon fomented a storm of controversy. He has not repeated that mistake.

Jesus said that the Pharisees' traditions had made void the Word of God. Though there are different interpretations of baptism, apparently the Lord has honored the faith in the various camps; for there are Christians in nearly all denominations. We shall see in our study that there is room for differences of interpretation which do not void the Word of God.

However, some teachings on this subject are erroneous, and practices of some denominations are not even in accord with their own beliefs. Also, the member congregations of a denomination often disagree on baptism. But where the Word of God has been faithfully taught, the Holy Spirit has produced children of God in spite of errors in doctrine. No one has a corner on the truth. We have to say as Paul did, "For our knowledge is imperfect and our prophecy is imperfect . . . Now I know in part." Praise God that the Holy Spirit can use any one of us even though our knowledge is imperfect.

The writer of the book of Hebrews indicated that water baptism is "an elementary doctrine of Christ." He bids his readers who are living on the "milk" of the Word to mature to "solid food." He bids his readers to leave the elementary doctrines of repentance from dead works, faith toward God, with instruction about baptism, the laying on of hands, the resurrection from the dead, and eternal judgment, and press on to maturity (Hebrews 5:11-6:3). Since the doctrine of water baptism is foundational, we must understand it.

I honestly desire that the Holy Spirit will take the things of Christ from His Word and bring that unity for which Jesus Christ prayed when He said, "That they may be one, even as we are one." I trust that this study will be used to bring understanding, acceptance, and a unity of fellowship within the household of faith, even though there may not be total agreement on this subject. I present this study with the desire that it may achieve the goal Paul set before the Philippians when he wrote:

So if there is any encouragement in Christ, any incentive of love, any participation in the Spirit, any affection and sympathy, complete my joy by being of the same mind, having the same love, being in full accord and of one mind. Do nothing from selfishness or conceit, but in humility count others better than yourselves. Let each of you look not only to his own interests, but also to the interests of others. Have this mind among yourselves, which you have in Christ Jesus (Philippians 2:1-5).

Discussion
1. To what extent can Christians compromise on doctrine to foster unity in the body of Christ?
2. Would it be feasible from time to time for a denomination to test its doctrinal statements against the Scriptures? Would it be beneficial to compare the doctrinal positions of differing denominations with your own and with the Scriptures?

1

What is the agency of the new birth?

"For by grace you have been saved through faith; *and this is not your own doing, it is the gift of God—not because of works, lest any man should boast" (Ephesians 2:8,9 RSV).*

"For I am not ashamed of the Gospel; it is the power of God for salvation to everyone who has faith" *(Romans 1:16 RSV).*

"They are justified by his grace as a gift, through the redemption which is in Christ Jesus, whom God put forward as an expiation by his blood, to be received by faith" *(Romans 3:24,25 RSV).*

"Because, if you confess with your lips that Jesus is Lord and believe in your heart that God raised him from the dead, you will be saved. For man believes with his heart *and so is justified, and he* confesses with his lips *and* so is saved" *(Romans 10:9,10 RSV).*

"So faith *comes from what is heard, and what is heard comes by the preaching of Christ" (Romans 10:17 RSV).*

In the third chapter of John's Gospel is what many hold to be the first recorded dissertation of Jesus in His public ministry. He is speaking to Nicodemus, a ruler of the Jews. Nicodemus was learned in the doctrines and teachings of the Pharisees, the orthodox and conservative segment of the Jewish faith.

This man came to Jesus one night and told Him, "Rabbi, we know that you are a teacher come from God; for no one can do these signs which you do, unless God is with Him."

Jesus answered Nicodemus, "Verily, verily, I say unto you, except a man be born anew, he cannot see the Kingdom of God."

Nicodemus questioned, "How can a man be born when he is old? Can he enter a second time into his mother's womb and be born?"

Jesus answered, "Verily, verily, I say unto you, except a man is born of water and spirit, he cannot enter the Kingdom of God. That which is born of the flesh is flesh, and that which is born of the Spirit is spirit. So marvel not that I say unto you, 'You must be born again'" (John 3:1-7).

These words are very dear to me because they were instrumental in my own conversion to Christianity. While I was still unconverted, practicing law in Seattle, Washington, my sister Jane came to my office one day and startled me with her confession, "Herb, I am born again. I have a new life in Jesus Christ. While I was visiting Mother, I met two missionaries who spoke to me about Jesus for three days. As a result, I confessed my sins and accepted Jesus Christ as my Savior. He has come into my life and has given me a new heart. I have been born again. And this is for you too, Herb. Jesus Christ is the Savior of the world, and He will save you if you will open your heart to Him."

I was sure my sister was suffering from religious delusions and switched the conversation to more mundane things as soon as I could.

10

Two weeks later she came to our home on a Saturday morning while my wife was out shopping. Jane opened her Bible and read me the words of Jesus in the third chapter of John. Then she began comparing me to Nicodemus, "You are just like Nicodemus, Herb. He was decent, respectable, educated and moral, but he was not born again. Jesus had to say to this educated and moral man, 'Except you are born again, you will never enter the Kingdom of God.' And that is what you need, Herb. You need to be born again."

But my mind did not accept what she was saying, for the natural mind does not receive the things of God. They are foolishness to it, for they are only discerned spiritually. I ended that conversation with explosive anger, but those words of Jesus spoken by my sister were indelibly inscribed upon my mind. Even though I diligently sought to erase them from my memory, I could not.

Six months later I had a dream in which, I believed, I was warned by God. This stirred me to seek God. My wife and I began regular church attendance, first in many churches, then in one where a man of God taught and preached the Word. Within seven months I came to repentance over my sin and sinfulness and came to Jesus Christ as Savior and Lord. This brought the sure mercies of Christ to me in a tangible way and I knew that I had been born anew. The heavens seemed opened to me in that experience, for I sensed the presence of a brilliant light that seemed to penetrate my whole being, lifting my guilt feelings and flooding my heart with the love of God. Tears of joy streamed down my face.

The day after this experience I called my sister Jane on the telephone, "Jane, this is Herb."

She screamed, "Herb, you've been converted."

I asked, "Who told you?"

And her reply, "Herb, I can tell it in your voice."

11

Having been a Christian for many years now, I know that the children of God have a gift of discernment which the Holy Spirit quickens for their use. I'm sure that gift enabled my sister to sense my new life in Christ.

In John 3 Jesus used emphatic words to declare the exclusive way of entering the Kingdom of God—*the new birth*. "Verily, verily, I say unto you," He started out. "*Except* a man be born again," and, "Marvel not that I say unto you, you *must* be born anew."

The new birth is an imperative. There is no other way. Entrance into His Kingdom, salvation, becoming a true disciple in the Kingdom, depends upon one being born anew. Unless one be born of water and spirit, he cannot enter the Kingdom of God.

Because they were important in my own conversion, I chose the words, *born of water and spirit,* as my thesis topic at Luther Theological Seminary. Note that I left out the definite article before the word, *spirit,* for the article does not appear in the original language, Greek. When translators put in a definite article, they unwittingly have become expositors, or interpreters, for the article does change the meaning of the text.

The purpose of my thesis was to gather and examine what major theologians from many denominations have held those words to mean. I found no less than nine major interpretations. All interpretations have reasonable and plausible foundations, both from Scripture and from rational thought.

One rather intriguing interpretation said that "born of water" refers to the physical birth, for the Greek word *ek,* which is generally translated "of," literally means "out of." Hence "born of water" could be translated "born out of water." This interpretation gathered its weight from the fact that every embryo in its mother's womb is encased in a sac of water. When birth takes place the sac of water breaks. And after speaking about being "born of water," Jesus said next, "That which is born of the flesh is flesh, and that which is born of Spirit is spirit." This statement implies that Jesus referred to physical birth when He spoke of being "born of water." There are two births, physical and spiritual. In this interpretation there is no reference to water baptism at all, and therefore, water baptism has nothing to do with the new birth. This was one of many plausible interpretations.

Martin Luther, however, with many other theologians, believed that the word *water* did refer to water baptism. John the Baptist was baptizing with water, and so was Jesus and His disciples. As a member of the Sanhedrin, the Seventy Elders, Nicodemus was likely responsible in part for the committee that had been sent out to John to find out the reason for his baptisms. It was logical, therefore, that Jesus in this conversation would answer that query in part.

Luther noted that Jesus spoke of being "born of water and spirit" with no definite article before the word *spirit*. Luther concluded that the Lord was not referring to the Holy Spirit but was using the general word *spirit*. Jesus used this word again in another statement, "The words that I have spoken to you are *spirit* and life" (John 6:63). The Word of God is spirit, and through the teaching and preaching of the Word of God, people come in to the new birth. Luther wrote:

Therefore, the words, "Except a man be born of water and spirit," are equivalent to saying, a person must be born anew by preaching the Gospel and the ordinance of baptism, by which the Holy Spirit operates. For by means of the Word he enlightens the heart and reveals God's wrath against sin; and, on the other hand, by showing us the grace of God

13

which has been promised for the sake of His Son, Christ, he so kindles our hearts that we begin to believe and soon turn to God, take comfort from His grace and call upon him. And in order to rouse and strengthen our faith he adds baptism as a sure sign, along with the Word, to show that he washes away and blots out our sins at all times, firmly to keep us for this grace and the gift of the Holy Spirit which he has promised us.*

Jesus spoke of the Word of God as the "good seed" which is sown into the hearts of men whereby they become the sons of the Kingdom (Matthew 13:24,38). Peter reminded Christians that "You have been born anew, not of perishable seed but of imperishable, through the living and abiding *Word of God*" (I Peter 1:23). James said it another way, "Of his own will he brought us forth by the *Word of truth* that we should be a kind of first fruits of his creatures" (1:18).

We make disciples by the teaching and preaching of the Word so that saving faith is born in their hearts. Paul said, "Faith comes by hearing and hearing by the *Word of God*" (Romans 10:17). The writer of the book of Hebrews notes the inner working of the Word of God in the believer's life, "*The Word of God* is living and active, sharper than any two-edged sword, piercing to the division of soul and spirit, of joints and marrow, and discerning the thoughts and intentions of the heart. And before him no creature is hidden, but all are open and laid bare to the eyes of him with whom we have to do" (Hebrews 4:12,13).

The Scriptures state that the new birth comes about by believing the Word of God concerning Jesus Christ as Savior and Lord. Paul wrote, "By grace you have

---

Lenker, J.N., Luther's Church Postils, 1907, vol. 12, page 432.

14

been saved through faith," "Believe in the Lord Jesus Christ and you will be saved," and "They are justified by His grace as a free gift, through the redemption which is in Christ Jesus, whom God put forward as an expiation by His blood, *to be received by faith*" (Ephesians 2:8, Acts 16:31, Romans 3:24,25).

John wrote, "As many as received him, who believed on his name, he gave power to become sons of God" (John 1:12). Here believing on Jesus Christ is equated with receiving Him, for if one truly believes on Jesus Christ as the Savior and Lord of all, he will receive Christ as his own Lord and Savior and be born again.

In this same discourse Jesus explains the new birth in terms of faith in "the Son of Man" who was lifted up even as Moses lifted up the serpent in the wilderness. Moses lifted up a brazen serpent so that any Israelite who had been bitten by poisonous snakes could look at the brazen serpent and be healed. There is the Gospel in a nut shell. The Lord Jesus Christ, the Son of Man, was lifted up on a cross where He atoned for the sins of the world, and anyone who looks up to Him with the eye of faith will be saved from the lethal poison of sin.

The Lord would have no misunderstanding of this very important matter of the new birth, for he goes on to say, "For God so loved the world that he gave his only son, that whosoever believes on him should not perish but have eternal life" (John 3:16). Again Jesus Christ defines the new birth in terms of faith in Himself as the one given by God for our salvation. He goes on to say, "For God sent the son into the world, not to condemn the world, but that the world might be saved through him. He who believes in him is not condemned; he who does not believe is condemned already, because he has not believed in the name of the only son of God" (John 3:17,18).

Jesus said to Nicodemus, "Do not marvel that I said

15

unto you, 'You must be born anew.' The wind blows where it wills, and you hear the sound of it, but you do not know whence it comes or whither it goes. So it is with every one who is born of the Spirit" (John 3:7,8). There is a mystery about the new birth like the mystery of the wind. When a seeking soul hears the teaching and preaching of the Word of God, he hears the sound of the words, but in a mysterious manner they become to him the very voice of God. He becomes aware that God is speaking to him personally. The Holy Spirit takes that Word and declares it to his innermost being. When he listens to that Word and responds to it in faith, the miracle of the new birth takes place in him and he knows the meaning of the Christmas hymn, *O Little Town of Bethlehem,* for it has happened to him. "How silently the wondrous gift is given! . . . No ear may hear His coming but . . . where meek souls will receive him, . . . Christ enters in."

Discussion

1. Why do unconverted church-going people want to be counted Christian when they really are not? Ignorance? Pride?

2. If the Word of God is the means to bring about salvation, what then is baptism?

3. Is faith a matter of having right knowledge? Is it mental assent to the truth? What is saving faith?

4. What are some of the ways besides being born again that people think will gain them acceptance with God and eternal life?

5. Are Scriptural passages used to support these ideas? Does the error of these people lie in their understanding of Scripture?

6. Or does their error lie in their understanding of the nature of God and the nature of man?

2

Baptism and salvation

"Baptism, which corresponds to this, now saves you, *not as a removal of dirt from the body but as an appeal to God for a clear conscience through the resurrection of Jesus Christ" (I Peter 3:21 RSV).*

"And now why do you wait? Rise and be baptized, and wash away your sins, *calling on his name" (Acts 22:16 RSV).*

"He who believes and is baptized *shall be* saved" *(Mark 16:16 RSV).*

"Jesus answered, 'Truly, truly, I say to you, unless one is born of water *and spirit, he cannot enter the Kingdom of God' " (John 3:5 RSV).*

"Husbands, love your wives, as Christ loved the church and gave himself up for her, that he might sanctify her, having cleansed her by the washing of water with the Word" *(Ephesians 5:25,26 RSV).*   ·

Peter said in his first letter, "Baptism now saves you" (I Peter 3:31). That is a true statement, but it is a half-truth. The verse continues, "Not as a removal of dirt from the body but as an appeal to God for a clear conscience through the resurrection of Jesus Christ."

Peter is saying that baptism saves you when you have a clear conscience through the resurrection of Jesus Christ. One can have a clear conscience through Christ only when he believes in Jesus Christ as his Savior and Lord. In other words, there must be the subjective condition of saving faith within the heart of the baptized person for this word, "Baptism now saves you," to be true. Without a heart trust in Jesus Christ, baptism will not save.

There are some similarities between baptism and circumcision. They are both initiatory rites. They both indicate a covenant relation between God and the individual. They both testify to faith in God and His promises and a resulting righteousness (Romans 4:11, Colossians 2:11,12).

The Bible is clear that Abraham had his salvation through faith and not through circumcision. Paul wrote, "Abraham believed in God, and it (his faith) was reckoned to him as righteousness." And then follows this word, "How then was it reckoned to him? Was it before or after he had been circumcised? It was not after but before he was circumcised" (Romans 4:3,10). Paul concludes by saying, "But the words, 'it was reckoned to him,' were written not for his sake alone, but for ours also. It will be reckoned to us who *believe* in him that raised from the dead Jesus our Lord, who was put to death for our trespasses and raised for our justification" (vs. 23-25). Faith was crucial for Abraham and faith is crucial for salvation in the New Testament era.

In the second chapter of Romans Paul refers to the circumcised Jew who did not keep the law, his "circumcision becomes uncircumcision" (v. 26). We can conclude that when a baptized person no longer has, or never had, a heart trust in Jesus Christ, his baptism then becomes "unbaptism," to coin a word. Paul explains,

"For he is not a real Jew who is one outwardly, nor is true circumcision something external and physical. He is a Jew who is one inwardly, and real circumcision is a matter of the heart, spiritual and not literal. His praise is not from men but from God" (Romans 2:28,29). Can we not say the same thing about baptism? A Christian is one who is inwardly spiritual, and real baptism is a matter of the heart. The Bible reveals that of all the circumcised Israelites only a remnant of them were truly God's people (Isaiah 10:22,23; Romans 9:27). Paul wrote, "For not all who are descended from Israel belong to Israel, and not all are children of Abraham because they are his descendants; but 'through Isaac shall your descendants be named.' This means that it is not the children of the flesh who are children of God, but the children of the promise are reckoned as descendants" (Romans 9:6-8). The children of the promise are those who believe inwardly as did Abraham. Though many Jews were circumcised, only those who had true faith were the children of God.

As it was with circumcision, so it is with baptism. There must be faith to validate the rite. Luther saw this truth. In his *Small Catechism,* where he defines the benefits of baptism, he wrote: "It is not the water, indeed, that does such great things, but the Word of God connected with the water, and our *faith which relies on that Word of God"* (pp. 18,19). Luther clearly saw that a subjective condition called *faith in the Word of God* was necessary for baptism to be effective.

The crossing of the Red Sea by the Israelites points up this union of faith and baptism. After they had escaped from Egypt, they were led by the Lord who appeared as a cloud by day and a pillar of fire by night. The Lord led them to the wrong side of the Red Sea. Egyptian soldiers pursued and surrounded them. When the Israelites saw their plight, they blamed God and Moses.

But Moses interceded for them and God told him what to do. Moses struck the waters of the Red Sea with his staff and the waters parted. He issued a command to his people, "Go forward!" They obeyed, trusting the mighty hand of God to hold back the walls of water, and they walked on the bottom of the sea. When they came up on the other side, the Scriptures reveal that they both feared and trusted in the Lord (Exodus 13,14).

Paul wrote of this experience, "I want you to know, brethren, that our fathers were all under the cloud, and all passed through the sea, and all were baptized into Moses in the cloud and in the sea, and all ate the same supernatural food and all drank the same supernatural drink. For they drank from the supernatural Rock which followed them and the Rock was Christ" (I Corinthians 10:1-4).

It was the Lord Jehovah that appeared to them in the form of a cloud by day and a pillar of fire by night. The words of Paul explicitly inform us that the Lord Jehovah was the preincarnate Christ. Note again the words of Paul. They were baptized unto Moses in the cloud (Christ) and in the sea (water). They exercised faith by answering the call of Moses to "Go forward!"

When Philip encountered the Ethiopian treasurer on his way to the city of Gaza, the Ethiopian was reading the Scriptures. Philip asked if he understood what he was reading.

"How can I, unless some one guides me?" replied the Ethiopian.

And from that Scripture, Philip told him the good news of salvation through Jesus Christ. Apparently Philip spoke of baptism, for as they were riding along the Ethiopian saw some water and said, "See, here is water! What is to prevent my being baptized?"

"If you believe with all your heart you may."

20

"I believe that Jesus Christ is the Son of God," he replied.

Thereupon Philip baptized the Ethiopian, who went on his way rejoicing (Acts 8:36-39). So we see the necessary ingredients, first faith in Jesus Christ, then baptism into His name.

The film, *The Godfather,* makes a travesty of the Christian faith. A gangleader was called the "godfather" because he was the sponsor at the baptism of a child who also grew up to be a gangleader. There was no sign of spirituality in that household whatsoever, and yet they clung to a traditional Christianity which included infant baptism.

I heard a story from a young man living in Minneapolis who worked as an auto mechanic. He was a Christian but his two coworkers were not. Both coworkers were quite profane and coarse. The Christian had shared the Gospel with these men several times without success.

However, one day they informed the Christian that they too had decided to become Christians. They enrolled in "the Pastor's class" in the church where both their wives attended. Not long after, they were baptized and confirmed in that church. But they still cursed and blasphemed God as before, with no outward sign of a change in their lives. They were baptized but not converted.

Many people in every land have been baptized and thus occupy the same position as the circumcised Jew, but are not walking in a faith relationship with Christ. Therefore, they do not have salvation. There are millions who have been baptized but never go to worship services and have no spiritual inclinations whatsoever. Jesus Christ said, "He who believes and is baptized shall be saved, but he who does not believe is condemned already because he does not believe" (Mark

16:16). Faith is the crucial issue. Jesus is saying that he who does not believe, even though he is baptized, is condemned already.

Discussion
1. Is baptism a converting rite?
2. Study Romans chapter 4 and answer these questions:
   vs. 1-8 What brought righteousness to Abraham?
   With what is this contrasted?
   vs. 9-12 What was the place of circumcision in Abraham's righteousness?
   What was its meaning and purpose?
   vs. 13-15 What is the relation between law and faith?
   vs. 16-25 Why did God select this means of giving righteousness to man?
3. What did Martin Luther believe was the operative condition to make baptism effective? What condition is given in I Peter 3:21?
4. When does God give power to become a son of God? John 1:12. Does a priest or pastor have this power to make someone a child of God? John 1:13, I Corinthians 3:5,6.

3

The benefits of baptism

"For in Christ Jesus you are all sons of God, through faith. For as many of you as were baptized into Christ have put on Christ" *(Galatians 3:26,27 RSV).*

"And Peter said unto them, 'Repent, and be baptized every one of you in the name of Jesus Christ for the forgiveness of your sins; *and you shall receive the gift of the Holy Spirit" (Acts 2:38 RSV).*

"Do you not know that all of us who have been baptized into Christ Jesus were baptized into his death? We were* buried *therefore with him by baptism into death, so that as Christ was raised from the dead by the glory of the Father, we too might* walk in newness of life" *(Romans 6:3,4 RSV).*

"And now why do you wait? Rise and be baptized, and wash away your sins, *calling on his name" (Acts 22:16 RSV).*

"For by one Spirit we were all baptized into one body—Jews or Greeks, slaves or free—and all were made to drink of one Spirit" *(I Corinthians 12:13 RSV).*

There are two extreme positions in Christendom concerning the merits of baptism. One says baptism is the means for the new birth, giving the recipient all spiritual graces, which then unfold in his walk before the Lord. The other says baptism is merely a sign or a seal, an act of obedience to the Lord's command, but it confers nothing. Many Christians take positions between these two extremes.

I have compared baptism to circumcision to make a valid point, but circumcision was part of the ceremonial law. Baptism is not in the same category. It is not just another rite which becomes a sign or a seal after one becomes a Christian. Water baptism, rightly understood, is part of the Gospel and belongs to salvation. Baptism is more than a rite; it is a means of grace.

As we saw in our last study, many are baptized but are not born again because they do not believe in Jesus Christ. But where there is faith in Jesus Christ, the Word of God and baptism effect the new birth. Baptism without faith does not bring salvation. But where there is faith there must be baptism. No one is counted a Christian in the book of Acts until he is baptized. Baptism is a concomitant to the preaching of the Gospel. Those who heard the Word were baptized immediately. The Philippian jailer was told, "Believe on the Lord Jesus Christ and you shall be saved." And that night he and his family were baptized. Jesus said, "He who believes and is baptized shall be saved," making baptism necessary for salvation.

Paul writes, "For in Christ Jesus you are all sons of God, through faith," and immediately adds, "For as many of you as were baptized into Christ have put on Christ" (Galatians 3:26,27). Receiving Christ as Savior by faith and being baptized into the name of the Father, Son, and Holy Spirit are considered by Paul as part of the same transaction. There may be a time lapse with baptism coming either before or after true heart faith, but it is apparent to me that God sees these as part of the same transaction.

Because baptism is a means of grace, it confers the sure mercies of Jesus Christ to those who have faith. Then all that is associated with salvation belongs to the believer who is baptized.

1. *The forgiveness of sins is associated with baptism.* Peter heard the cry of thousands of Jews on the day of Pentecost, "Brethren, what shall we do?"

His answer was, "Repent and be baptized every one of you in the name of Jesus Christ *for the forgiveness of your sins*" (Acts 2:38).

Ananias said to Paul after Paul's conversion, "And now why do you wait? Rise and be baptized, and *wash away your sins,* calling on His name" (Acts 22:16). Paul wrote how Jesus Christ loved the Church and gave Himself for her, "That he might sanctify her, having *cleansed her by the washing of water with the word*" (Ephesians 5:26). When an unbeliever who has heard the Word of God repents of his sins, calls upon the Lord and believes His pardoning Word, he has total forgiveness; yet the salvation of that person has its completion in the act of baptism. If that person should refuse baptism, at that point his faith would not be complete.

2. *Salvation is attributed to baptism.* We refer again to Peter's words, "Baptism now saves you." We understand that baptism saves us only when we have faith towards Jesus Christ. The words of Jesus also apply here, "He who believes and is baptized shall be saved" (I Peter 3:21, Mark 16:16).

3. *Baptism brings one into union with Christ.* I quote again the words of Paul in Galatians 3:27, "For in Christ Jesus you are all sons of God through faith; for as many of you as were baptized into Christ have put on

25

Christ." In the sixth chapter of Romans Paul states that a person who is baptized into Christ is united to Christ in His death and resurrection (vv. 4-11). The same truth is expressed by Paul also in Colossians 2:11-13.

4. *Baptism is a condition for receiving the gift of the Holy Spirit.* I know there are differences of opinion here, for no one can be a Christian unless he has the Spirit of Christ within him (Romans 8:9). Every Christian has the indwelling Holy Spirit. But on the day of Pentecost when that great crowd gathered at the sound of a rushing mighty wind and the disciples were speaking in other tongues, Peter exhorted the listeners, "Repent and be baptized every one of you for the forgiveness of your sins; and you shall receive the gift of the Holy Spirit, for the promise is to you and to your children and to all that are afar off, every one whom the Lord our God calls to Him" (Acts 2:38,39).

Peter with the other disciples had received the Holy Spirit on the day of resurrection, for Jesus had breathed upon them and said, "Receive the Holy Spirit." This was for their salvation, that they might become the sons of God. This was the Spirit of God coming to indwell them. However, immediately after, Jesus told these same disciples that they would receive power *after that the Holy Ghost has come upon them.* They were told to wait in Jerusalem for the promise of the Father. At that time they would receive power to witness and to carry out His commission.

The Holy Spirit was not yet given in this way, for Jesus had not yet been glorified. The condition for this enduement of power was the glorification of Jesus Christ (John 7:37-39). The disciples had already received the indwelling Spirit of Christ and were sons of God, but they later received the Holy Spirit who came *upon them.* This second event was manifested by their speaking in other tongues as the Spirit of God gave ut-

26

terance, by their great joy and by a strong wind.

Peter informed his Pentecost audience that they could receive the same power, the same *promise of the Father,* after they had become Christians through repentance and Christian baptism. And this pattern is evidenced throughout the book of Acts: first the unbelievers repented of their sins, received Christ as Savior, were baptized with water, and then came the gift of the Holy Spirit. The Spirit came either by the laying on of hands or the preaching of the Word.

There was one exception: the sovereign move of God with Cornelius and his household. They received the anointing power of the Holy Spirit, evidenced by the gifts of tongues and prophecy, before they had received baptism.

Without faith, baptism accomplishes nothing. But with faith in the heart of the recipient, all that is attributed to salvation through faith in Christ is likewise attributed to baptism.

That baptism is a means of grace has been evidenced by the power of the Holy Spirit accompanying this ordinance, as many can testify. In my ministry as a parish pastor over a period of nine years, I officiated at many baptismal services in which I became aware of the presence of the Lord and the power of the Holy Spirit. As I served a church in Anchorage, Alaska, one of my members came to my office to inform me that he had decided not to baptize his baby girl. He had read many books on the subject of baptism and had a firm conviction that baptism was only for those who were mature and had come to a personal faith in Jesus Christ. He was convinced that it was wrong to baptize infants and children.

When this child was four months old, she became violently ill with colic. The doctor feared that the child would not live. Then the mother became assertive and wanted the baby baptized. The husband succumbed to her convictions. Though not fully convinced that this was a right decision, he and his wife came to my office and requested baptism.

The baptism took place on the following day during a Sunday morning service. As I poured the baptismal waters upon the head of that child, there was an obvious reaction. Her arms fell in a symbol of release and peace and her body relaxed noticeably. The child was instantly healed of colic. At that time I was not in the healing ministry. The child was not baptized in order to be healed. And I refer to this incident because it was so obvious to me, the parents and members of my congregation, that the Holy Spirit moved upon that child in that baptismal service.

I have noted in other services the love and joy of the Lord coming upon the person baptized, especially on older children and adults who could witness to their experience. In a baptismal service where believers come together in the name of Jesus Christ, speak and share His Word, pray and call upon the Lord, the presence of the Lord is there. Who knows all that does happen, intangibly and unseen, when a person is baptized?

Another incident where I was privileged to see the work of the Holy Spirit in baptism was in San Jose, California. I was holding meetings in Calvary Community Church and witnessed a baptismal service one Saturday evening. Over a dozen adults were being baptized by immersion. As soon as they came up from the water, the pastor laid hands upon them and said, "Receive the Holy Ghost." They immediately spoke in tongues, every one of them. Some of them spoke in tongues as soon as they came out of the water before the pastor could lay his hands on them. Now this is not the usual experience, but as I learned from their pastor, they had been instructed that as soon as they were baptized they could receive the gift of the Holy Spirit. Because they expected to receive the Holy Spirit, they did.

I mention this to stress that baptism is not merely a rite, not some seal or sign, but a means to the sure mercies that are in Christ Jesus our Lord, a signal part of our salvation in the Kingdom of God.

Discussion

1. Is baptism necessary for salvation? If yes, are there any exceptions? Is the child of a believer lost if he dies without baptism?

2. Is faith necessary for salvation? Are there any exceptions?

3. Why do you think God instituted baptism? What was its primary significance in the early Church?

4. The Israelites were baptized into Moses in the sea and in the cloud (I Corinthians 10:1-4). What conditions did they fulfill before their baptism? Are there similar conditions today?

5. What makes baptism a means of grace? Objectively. Subjectively.

6. Where there is faith in Christ, what does baptism confer?

7. What two conditions did Peter give on the day of Pentecost for receiving the gift of the Holy Spirit?

4

Does a child need salvation?

"Behold, I was brought forth in iniquity, *and in sin did my mother conceive me" (Psalm 51:5 RSV).*

"If we say we have no sin, *we deceive ourselves, and the truth is not in us" (I John 1:8 RSV).*

"For I know that nothing good dwells within me, that is, in my flesh. I can will what is right, but I cannot do it. For I do not do the good I want, but the evil I do not want is what I do. Now if I do what I do not want, it is no longer I that do it, but sin which dwells within me. *So I find it to be a law that when I want to do right, evil lies close at hand. For I delight in the law of God, in my inmost self, but I see in my members another law at war with the law of my mind and making me captive to the law of* sin which dwells in my members. *Wretched man that I am! Who will deliver me from this body of death?" (Romans 7:18-24 RSV).*

"For as by one man's disobedience many were made sinners, *so by one man's obedience many will be made righteous" (Romans 5:19 RSV).*

We can easily see how the matters of faith and baptism apply to an adult. But where does a child fit into the scheme of God's salvation? Can a child have faith?

30

Does a child need salvation? Christians disagree on these questions. Let's see what the Scriptures say.

The Christian Church has generally believed that the taint of original sin is from conception. The Bible defines what we are by nature. "By nature we are children of wrath, like the rest of mankind" (Ephesians 2:3). Paul spoke of that nature with which all are born as descendants of Adam. The divine nature is something which is imparted only to those who truly believe in Jesus Christ (II Peter 1:3,4; John 1:12).

The Bible reveals that the natural mind of man "does not receive the things of God, for they are folly to him, and he is not able to understand them because they are spiritually discerned" (II Corinthians 2:14). And that is why Jesus said "that which is born of the flesh is flesh and that which is born of the Spirit is spirit. Do not marvel that I say unto you, you must be born again" (John 3:6,7). By our natural birth we have a bent toward sin. We are naturally afraid of God. We avoid God and find our peace in going our own way, doing our own thing, a law unto ourselves.

David said, "Behold I was brought forth in iniquity, and in sin did my mother conceive me" (Psalm 51:5). From the context it is obvious that David was concerned about his own sinfulness and was not referring to the act that brought about his conception. We are brought forth in a state of sin which the Scriptures refer to as "the natural man," "flesh," "our old self." John wrote, "If we say we have no sin, we deceive ourselves, and the truth is not in us" (I John 1:8). Paul explains it in Romans 7:

> We know that the law is spiritual; but I am carnal, sold under sin. I do not understand my actions. For I do not do what I want, but I do the very thing I hate. Now if I do what I do not

31

want, I agree that the law is good. So then it is no longer I that do it, but *sin that dwells within me.* For I know that nothing good dwells within me, that is, in my flesh. I can will what is right, but I cannot do it. For I do not do the good that I want, but the evil I do not want is what I do. Now if I do what I do not want, it is no longer I that do it, *but sin which dwells within me* (7:14-20).

Adam was made in the image of God, but he and his wife disobeyed the specific instruction of God and ate the forbidden fruit. As a result their natures were corrupted. They who had been in fellowship with God were now afraid of Him, hid from Him.

We read in the Scriptures concerning their progeny: "When Adam had lived 130 years he became the father of a son *in his own likeness, after his image*" (Genesis 5:3,4). Adam was created in the image of God, but his son was born in the image of his sinful father. Paul informs us that condemnation and death came to all men because of Adam's sin. "Because of one man's sin the many (meaning the human race) were made sinners" (Romans 5:15,18,19). When Adam sinned, the seed of the human race which was in him became contaminated with a condition called sin.

A child not only has original sin, but because of original sin, he sins on his own account. John stated, "If we say we have no sin (here he refers to original sin), we deceive ourselves . . . if we say we have not sinned (here he refers to sin as an act of disobedience), we make God a liar" (I John 1:8,10). "All have sinned and come short of the glory of God," Paul writes. "There are none righteous, no not so many as one," he states again (Romans 3:10). You do not have to teach a child to be angry, jealous or selfish—these traits appear naturally and frequently in all children.

Some hold that a child cannot sin because he lacks the understanding to be held morally accountable. But where is the scriptural foundation for this view? And when does a child become morally accountable? A child is born with a conscience, with the moral law written upon his heart, and he experiences guilt very early in his life. A toddler can experience the peace of forgiveness from the guilt of sin. As a pastor and a father, I have seen this very thing happen in children three and four years of age. The Word of God is all-inclusive when it speaks about original sin and the acts of sin.

If, as some say, a child is saved because he is a child, whether the reasoning be that the child is in a state of innocence or morally unaccountable, when does that child become lost? When does that child become morally accountable? Does this happen during puberty?

If children cannot sin, then the logical conclusion is that all children, even of heathens, are saved. And if they are saved, what a terrible penalty children pay for growing up. But this view is not in accord with the Scriptures. A child needs salvation like any other member of the human race.

The Scriptures speak of both sin and salvation as all-inclusive. "God so loved the world." "God was in Christ reconciling the world." "One has died for all." Jesus Christ is the Lamb of God who took away the sin of the world. Sin is all-inclusive because it involves everyone. Salvation is all-inclusive because it is available to all.

The new birth is the exclusive way of salvation, for the Lord holds all morally accountable, even the little, little child. The words of Jesus Christ, "Except a man be born again, he cannot see the Kingdom of God," include children as well as grownups. Only in Christ Jesus does one become a new creation (II Corinthians 5:17).

33

One is placed in Christ through the new birth. John used that exclusive and inclusive *all* when he wrote, "But to *all* who receive him, who believe on his name, he gave the power to become children of God" (John 1:12). "He who believes and is baptized shall be saved," and that is the way of salvation for children as well as for adults.

Paul, in writing about a marriage where one parent is a believer and the other is not, said that if the unbeliever was content to live with the believer, he should be allowed to do so. Paul said that the unbeliever is sanctified by the believer and states that: "Otherwise your children would be unclean, but as it is they are holy" (I Corinthians 7:12-14). This verse indicates that children of unbelievers are unclean and, therefore, need salvation. The word which means unclean in this verse is the same word used to describe an unclean demon. The word appears again in Ephesians 5:5 where Paul states that no unclean person shall inherit the Kingdom of God. What do these verses do to the theology of those who hold that children of heathen are saved because they are children?

So we see that children are sinful and must be born again. They have inherited the nature of Adam and must be made new creatures in Jesus Christ.

Discussion
1. Is a child saved because it is a child? If so, when does such a child become lost? How do your views on the first two questions affect your view of your church's efforts to win children to the Lord?
2. Can a child sin? At what age?
3. When does a child become morally accountable? Does a child have a conscience? Support your answers with Scripture.
4. Does a child need salvation?

5

Can a child have faith?

"Yet thou art he who took me from the womb; Thou didst make me trust when I was upon my mother's breasts. I was cast upon thee from the womb; Thou art my God since my mother bare me" (Psalm 22:9,10; 71:5,6 ASV).

"But when Jesus saw it he was indignant, and said to them, 'Let the children come to me, do not hinder them; for to such belongs the kingdom of God. Truly, I say to you, whoever does not receive the kingdom of God like a child shall not enter it.' And he took them in his arms and blessed them, laying his hands upon them" (Mark 10:14-16 RSV).

"And calling to him a child, he put him in the midst of them, and said, 'Truly, I say to you, unless you turn and become like children, you will never enter the kingdom of heaven. Whoever humbles himself like this child, he is the greatest in the kingdom of heaven. Whoever receives one such child in my name receives me; but whoever causes one of these little ones who believe in me to sin, it would be better for him to have a great millstone fastened round his neck and to be drowned in the depth of the sea' " (Matthew 18:3-6 RSV).

"For the unbelieving husband is consecrated through his wife, and the unbelieving wife is consecrated through her husband. Otherwise your children would be unclean, but as it is they are holy" (I Corinthians 7:14 RSV).

"Fathers, do not provoke your children to anger, but bring them up *in the discipline and instruction of the Lord" (Ephesians 6:4 RSV).*

Many Christians believe that a child cannot repent, cannot believe and, therefore, is excluded from the call of the Gospel. These Christians misunderstand what the Bible means when it speaks of faith. Paul writes, "With the heart a man believes unto righteousness" (Romans 10:10). Some people have knowledge about the things of the kingdom of God, but do not have saving faith because "their hearts are far from God." A person may have mental knowledge of Jesus Christ, but lack a heart trust in Jesus because he has not been born of the Spirit.

When we speak about the faith of adults, we usually think of three elements of faith: knowledge, commitment and trust. Paul writes, "God desires that all men shall come to the knowledge of the truth and be saved" (I Timothy 2:4). I know what that verse meant to me. I had to come to the knowledge of my own lostness, my sinfulness, and then come to the knowledge of Jesus Christ, His atoning death, and His resurrection for my justification.

But this knowledge in itself was insufficient for my salvation. There was the matter of commitment or decision. One day I called upon the Lord, confessing my sinfulness and my faith in the atoning work of Jesus Christ on the cross for me. The Holy Spirit then worked the miracle of the new birth in me. In my heart grew a trust in the Lord Jesus. But all the knowledge I had gained prior to my commitment was only preparatory.

The crucial ingredient of an adult faith is trust, involving something of the heart, the inner man, the spirit of man. Paul prayed that Christians might be given a spirit of wisdom and of revelation in the knowledge of God, having the eyes of their hearts enlightened. His prayer indicates that the inner man can receive knowledge as does the mind, that there might be a heart trust in the Lord (Ephesians 1:16,17).

As a parish pastor I was called to minister to a woman who had been cruelly beaten by her husband. She lay unconscious for twelve days. When she regained consciousnes, she had mind damage, with only fleeting moments of rational thought. Later she was committed to a mental hospital. But before that time I had opportunities to minister to her and found that same inner resistance to the Word of God that I found in unbelievers generally. I learned that she had a Sunday School background and that she had memorized Psalm 23 and the Lord's Prayer. I used these words of Scripture, and after many sessions with her, I had her pray after me words of confession and faith. From that moment on, I noted the resistance was gone; a peace had come to her inner being, an openness to the Gospel message, even though she still suffered serious mental damage and could not cope with reality. I refer to this to emphasize that the important feature of faith is heart trust, a spirit open to Jesus.

Obviously, a child cannot have the same mental knowledge an adult can, but a child can have heart trust in the Lord. David had this trust as a child. "But thou art he who took me from the womb, and didst make me trust when I was upon my mother's breast. I was cast upon thee from the womb. Thou art my God since my mother bore me" (Psalm 22:9,10). The Hebrew word *batach,* which is translated in the above verse as

37

"trust," is translated "hope" in the King James version, and "didst make me trust" in the American Standard version. A basic word in respect to salvation, it is used over one hundred times in that context. It is a strong word and literally means "to lean on" or "to have confidence in." Translators generally give it the rendering of "trust."

In Psalm 22:4,5 for example, David writes, "In thee our fathers trusted; they trusted, and thou didst deliver them. To thee they cried, and were saved; in thee they trusted, and were not disappointed." Every word translated "trust" or "trusted" is the same Hebrew word *batach*. So I conclude that when David said that the Lord made him trust when he was upon his mother's breast, he was speaking about saving heart trust.

David used the same word in Psalm 71:5,6, "For thou, O Lord, art my hope, my trust, O Lord, from my youth. Upon thee I have trusted from my birth; thou art he who took me from my mother's womb." Because David had God-fearing parents, was in the household of faith, he was brought into covenant relationship with God through the rite of circumcision.

Other verses in the Old Testament indicate that children are within the purview of God's salvation. When God speaks to the "household of Jacob" and to "all the remnant of the house of Israel," He says, "Who have been borne by me from your birth, carried from the womb." God extended providential care to the Israelites from their earliest childhood (Isaiah 46:3). Isaiah could say, "The Lord called me from the womb, from the body of my mother he named my name" (Isaiah 49:1). The Lord spoke to Jeremiah and said, "Before I formed you in the womb, I knew you, and before you were born I consecrated you; I appointed you a prophet to the nations" (Jeremiah 1:5). We know that Jeremiah had a godly father, Hilkiah, who was the

High Priest in Israel. Both Isaiah and Jeremiah were in the household of faith.

The New Testament definitely includes children in salvation. Jesus said, "Let the children come unto me and forbid them not; for to such belongs the kingdom of God. Truly I say unto you, whoever does not receive the kingdom of God like a child shall not enter it" (Mark 10:14,15). Again Jesus said, "Truly I say to you, unless you turn and become like children, you will never enter the kingdom of heaven. Whoever humbles himself like this child, he is the greatest in the kingdom of heaven. Whoever receives one such child in my name receives me; but whoever causes one of these little ones who believe in me to sin (or stumble), it would be better for him to have a great millstone fastened round his neck and to be drowned in the depth of the sea" (Matthew 18:3-6).

The Greek word *paidion* that Jesus uses for child and children literally means a little child that is carried, thus a babe. Jesus is saying that little children belong to the kingdom of God, not by birth, but as candidates. They are examples to adults of humility and receptivity, and they can have faith in Jesus Christ. In speaking about little children, Jesus does not refer to mental knowledge, but to the important ingredient of faith— heart trust.

A careful study of both the Old and New Testaments will reveal that the anointing of the Holy Spirit for service comes upon those who have a true faith in God. On the day of Pentecost, Peter let his hearers know that they first had to repent and be baptized before they could receive the gift of the Holy Spirit. And Jesus said that the condition for receiving the anointing of the Spirit was believing on him (John 7:38,39). But John the Baptist received the anointing of the Holy Spirit from his mother's womb, indicating to me that there must have been a faith relationship with the Lord, even before he was born. I cannot understand this, but I can believe it. John the Baptist had believing parents, and they were both "filled with the Holy Spirit" (Luke 1:41,67). I know of many children who have been filled with the Holy Spirit at an early age.

I recall the testimony of a Lutheran pastor who relates that his child had this experience on the very day that he himself received the anointing of the Holy Spirit. On going to bed that night, his youngest son, two years of age, was restless and could not sleep. Several times he came to his father's bedside and pulled on the blankets. Each time the father got out of bed and put him back to bed. But again he came, and this time he said to his father, "Dad, I can't sleep."

"Why can't you sleep?" the father asked.

"The wind is blowing! The wind is blowing!" the little lad kept saying again and again.

The father realized that something spiritual was happening to his child, for there was no literal wind blowing that night. Thereupon he took the child in his arms and laid his hand upon the small head, asking the Father in Jesus' name to baptize his child in the Holy Spirit. The father soon heard that child muttering strange syllables.

The next morning at the breakfast table, amid the normal jabberings of the child, again came those strange syllables. The parents realized that their son had received the anointing of the Holy Spirit, for he was obviously speaking in another tongue! This child was in the household of faith. He belonged to God. He had been brought to the Lord in baptism. He believed in Jesus Christ. He was anointed with the Holy Spirit. "Of such is the Kingdom of God." "Your sons and daughters shall prophesy!"

Believing parents know that salvation is the most

precious of all gifts. Before their child is born, they will surround that child with their prayers. Jesus said that children are examples of receptivity. It is common knowledge among those working for the salvation of the lost, that the older a person becomes, the more difficult it is to reach that person for Christ. Conversely, the younger the person, the easier it is to reach him for the Kingdom.

As a parish pastor, I knew this to be true; the younger the child, the more receptive that child was. It seems to me that the Scriptures teach that a child in a believer's womb is the epitome of receptivity!

While in Iowa, I was instrumental in leading a young couple with two children to Christ. Later they had two more children. While the mother carried each of these children, it was my privilege to lay hands upon her, praying not only for her, but for her unborn child. Both parents were astonished to note the difference in the two children born to them after they had become Christians. They said the last two were like doves. And I have heard the same testimony from many others.

Believing parents, and in particular, fathers, are exhorted to bring up their children "in the nurture and the admonition of the Lord" (Ephesians 6:4). The Lord's command to the household of Israel in respect to children was: "And these words which I command you this day shall be upon your heart and you shall teach them diligently to your children, and shall talk of them when you sit in your house, and when you walk by the way, and when you lie down, and when you rise" (Deuteronomy 6:6,7). And Solomon's words were, "Train up a child in the way he should go, and when he is old he will not depart from it" (Proverbs 22:6).

You cannot nurture a dead thing, for the word presupposes that there is life there. When does this heart trust come to a child? Who knows but the Lord.

Can a child have faith? Again I look to some personal experiences in the parish ministry. We desperately needed an awakening in the parish I was serving in Anchorage, Alaska. It began with children! The second summer of that ministry, we held a family Bible camp. But the adults were wary and fearful, and they stayed home. With the exception of a few workers, the 150 campers were children.

The first evening of the camp, I had these children fill out a questionnaire about their faith in Jesus Christ as Savior and Lord, the forgiveness of sins and assurance of salvation. The fourth question was, "Are you sure you are a Christian?" with a multiple choice answer: "I am," "I am not," or, "I am not sure."

A nine-year-old girl in the front row began to cry convulsively. In seeking to help her I found that her problem was with the fourth question. She was not sure that she was a Christian. It was a simple matter to speak to her about her sin, forgiveness through Jesus Christ, and then to have her invite Jesus into her life. Peace came to her immediately, and she stood and gave a radiant testimony to her newfound joy in Christ's salvation. Each succeeding year at our camps, she testified of how she found peace with God at the first camp. Today she is an active Christian, married to a pastor, serving the Lord.

That same evening many other children who had the same problem with the fourth question were given the same help. Before the week was over, every child in that camp, many of them only five and six years of age, had an assured faith in Christ. When they went home, their parents were surprised by the new spirituality of their children. That fall a revival broke out among the adults. No doubt the witness of their own children at home was partially responsible.

Discussion

1. What does it mean to believe with your heart?
2. Is it possible for an adult to believe with his heart and yet lack mental knowledge? How about a child, an infant, an unborn child?
3. What can a Christian parent do to help his child grow up in the Lord to faith?
4. How great a responsibility does a Christian parent have if his child does not become a Christian?
5. How effective is a program of child evangelism that makes no attempt at winning the child's parents also?
6. When a child is brought to Christ, is a follow-up program more important or less important than when an adult comes to the Lord?

6

Children and baptism

"For the promise is to you and to your children and to all that are far off, every one whom the Lord our God calls to him" (Acts 2:39 RSV).

". . .The Lord opened her heart to give heed to what was said by Paul. And when she was baptized, with her household, she besought us saying, 'If you have judged me to be faithful to the Lord, come to my house and stay. . .' " (Acts 16:14-15 RSV).

"And he took them the same hour of the night, and washed their wounds, and he was baptized at once, with all his family " (Acts 16:33 RSV).

"(I did baptize also the household of Stephanas, beyond that I do not know whether I baptized any one else)" (I Corinthians 1:16 RSV).

"And when the time came for their purification according to the law of Moses, they brought him. . .to the Lord (as it is written in the law of the Lord, 'Every male that opens the womb shall be called holy to the Lord') and to offer a sacrifice according to what is said in the law of the Lord, 'a pair of turtledoves or two young pigeons' " (Luke 2:22-24 RSV).

44

Jesus commanded us to go and make disciples, baptize them and teach them. A disciple is a follower of Christ who has a heart trust in Jesus as Lord and God. A child can have heart trust in the Lord, especially when he is in the household of faith. We are commanded to baptize disciples. Should we not then baptize believing children? We have the command to teach our children, to "bring up our children in the nurture and admonition of the Lord." If we obey the one command, should we not obey the other?

A ten-year-old girl who attended our Sunday School in Anchorage, Alaska, came to me after church services, crying. Her Sunday School teacher had led her to a personal faith in Jesus Christ.

"What is the matter? Why are you crying?" I asked.

"Every Sunday morning when we are in Church," she replied, "I hear those words, 'He who believes and is baptized shall be saved,' and, pastor, I am not baptized." She was referring to a verse given as part of the absolution every Sunday morning in a Lutheran church.

I knew that her parents seldom attended any church, but I informed her that I would talk the matter over with them. They gladly gave me permission to baptize their daughter and came to the baptismal service. They permitted the girl's Sunday School teacher and my wife to be her sponsors. I do not recall seeing anyone with more joy in receiving baptism.

When an adult comes to Christ the usual order of the steps in conversion is first repentance, next faith in Jesus Christ as Savior and Lord, and then baptism. That was the order for the ten-year-old girl. But how about a baby? Repentance, mind faith and knowledge are not there. But where one or both of the parents are believers and they request baptism for their child, should the child be baptized?

In the Old Testament circumcision was for the

household of faith, and my conviction is that baptism is for the household of faith, although I do respect the conviction of others who disagree. This became my conviction as a parish pastor and it still is. Everytime we held a baptismal service in the congregations that I served, I announced, "Baptism is for the household of faith; for believers and their children." It wasn't long before everyone knew what I meant by those words.

I required that couples who wanted baptism for their children come for a personal interview. After a cordial time of general conversation, I would ask, "Why do you want your child baptized?" I received some very strange answers to that one. After clarification of the meaning of baptism, I would let them know that baptism is for believers and their children. To the question, "Are you a believer?" I would usually get an affirmative answer. But I learned to ask a question like this: "What does it mean to you when you say you are a believer?"

A person who knows Jesus as his personal Savior can confess that faith, but when he doesn't, his answer always involves religious performance, like, "Well, I go to church. I was baptized and went to Sunday School. My parents were good Christians and that is the way we were brought up, etc., etc."

In my personal interviews I did not try to embarrass people but made an honest effort to help them into a true faith. In many cases, before the interview was over, both mother and father called upon the Lord, opening their hearts to receive Him. In other cases where it was obvious they were not ready for such a prayer, I suggested that the parents enroll in the "Pastor's Class," where they would receive instruction on the way of salvation. And when the parents came to Christ, then we would baptize their children. Only in a few instances would parents storm out of my office because of the embarrassment at facing the question of their own salvation.

And what a joy to baptize their children after they had come to a personal faith in Jesus Christ. Some of them gave a personal testimony at the time of baptism. In this one parish in Anchorage, we had many couples in military service come to us seeking baptism for their children. (Anchorage had 35,000 soldiers quartered there.) What a joy to share Christ with the parents and lead them into a saving knowledge of Christ. So this became a fruitful occasion to fish for the souls of men and women as well as of their children.

And with my practice on baptism I saw the Scriptures agreeing. Peter, on the day of Pentecost, told that crowd of people who were cut to the heart over the guilt of their sin, "Repent and be baptized everyone of you for the remission of your sins; and you shall receive the gift of the Holy Spirit, for the promise is to you and to your children" (Acts 2:38,39).

Peter was addressing Jews who were already in covenant relationship with God through circumcision. They knew that salvation was for the household of faith in the Old Covenant, and would naturally question whether the same would be true in the New Covenant. Peter anticipated their query—salvation was for them and for their children.

What was the practice of the early Church as we see it in the book of Acts? We do not have all the details, but there are some specifics as to the household of faith. In Philippi Paul met a woman by the name of Lydia who was a "worshipper of God." According to the report of her conversion, "The Lord opened her heart to give heed to what was said by Paul. And when she was baptized, *with her household,* she besought us, saying, 'If you have judged me to be faithful to the Lord, come to my house and stay' " (Acts 16:14,15). Nothing is said

47

about who were included in that household, and we cannot say whether she had children, but all there were baptized. And this was done because after she became a believer, the others were in the household of faith.

On another occasion Paul and Silas told the Philippian jailer, "Believe in the Lord Jesus Christ, and you will be saved, *you and your household*." And the report continues, "And they spoke the Word of the Lord to him and to all that were in his house. And he took them the same hour of the night, and washed their wounds, and he was baptized at once, with all his family" (literally from the Greek, "he and all his.") (Acts 16:31-34). "He and all his" is a Greek expression meaning his family and presupposes there were children. If Paul had been against baptizing them, then that word would have been added.

Paul in his letter to the Corinthians stated that it wasn't his practice to baptize the converts. He indicated that he had baptized Crispus and Gaius, and then as an afterthought he wrote, "I did baptize also *the household* of Stephanas" (I Corinthians 1:16). Again we have baptism for the household of faith.

A child born into the household of faith has a tremendous advantage over one born to unbelievers. He not only has the benefit of his parents' prayers, but also the sanctifying influence of the Holy Spirit which indwells the parents. And such a child should learn to pray and call upon the Lord from the time he learns to talk. If the parents take their responsibility seriously, that child will be under the nurture and admonition of the Lord all his growing days. The Word of God reveals a salvation for households. In that salvation is baptism in water and into Christ, for in baptism one is baptized into Christ with the accompaniment of water. "He who believes and is baptized shall be saved," our Lord said, and baptism is for the entire household of faith.

Jesus, as a child of eight days, was brought to the temple for the rite of circumcision. When He was forty days of age, His mother came again to the temple with Jesus, and there made a sin offering for her child. Under the Old Covenant every first born male child was "holy unto the Lord" and had to be brought to the Lord to be redeemed through the shedding of the blood of an innocent substitute (Exodus 13:2,13-15; Leviticus 12:2-8; Luke 2:22-24). Jesus was in the household of faith, with a believing father and mother. He was brought into covenant relationship with God by the rite of circumcision, and then redeemed through the shed blood of a turtle dove when He was but forty days of age.

Children in the New Covenant who are in the household of faith are likewise *holy* unto the Lord, as we have already seen from the Word of God (I Corinthians 7:14). Parents can bring their children to redeem them, by baptizing them into the Lord Jesus Christ, whereby they will have a union with Him in His death (Romans 6:4-6). Thus they too will be redeemed by the shedding of blood, the only blood that avails in this day, the blood of Jesus Christ. Peter speaks of believers in the New Covenant as those who have been redeemed with the precious blood of Christ, a lamb without blemish and without spot (I Peter 1:18,19).

Interestingly, in most denominations where children are baptized, they are baptized after they are about six weeks of age, or about forty days old. That was the age of Jesus when He was brought to the Lord to be redeemed.

In my own home I witnessed how the Spirit of God worked out salvation for both of our boys. Through the insistence of my wife, who had been raised in a devoted Lutheran home and church, both of our boys were baptized as infants in a Lutheran church. This was part of a premarital understanding, my wife asking for the right to baptize any children born of our marriage and to send them to a Lutheran Sunday School. At that time I was agnostic, and to avoid arguments I gave consent, thinking that "a little religion would hurt nobody."

When I became a seeking soul, my oldest boy Alton was about six years of age. He had had very little contact with Sunday School or church, and when I insisted that he go with us to church, I found stubborn resistance. When we took him there, he would not go into a class unless I went with him. It was embarrassing for me to sit with him for three consecutive Sundays in a class of about ten other boys and their teacher, when at the time I was not a Christian myself. I was relieved on the fourth Sunday when we went to class and my boy said to me, "Dad, what are you doing here?" I realized that now he was embarrassed to have me along. But his heart was not in this new routine, and every Sunday morning we had a hassle getting him ready to go.

However, shortly after I became a Christian, Alton began to change. Either my wife or I read Bible stories to him and prayed with him. One evening I took my turn, reading a story about heaven and the ultimate victory around the great white throne. Afterward I prayed and Alton prayed. I noted a new seriousness in his prayer and a moving in his emotions.

After he was through he said, "Dad, it is so light in here. It is like heaven is open." He had opened his heart to Jesus and the Light of the World, Jesus Christ, had come in. No problem of getting him ready for Sunday School or church after that. Al has been a Christian ever since and today is an elder in his church.

My youngest son Doug was only a year old when I began my quest, and he was sixteen months when I opened my heart to have heaven's glory come streaming in. When I picked him up that night and walked the floor with him, I knew that the glory that had come to me had come to him too. There was a fellowship in the Spirit between my own heart and my son that only those who have experienced it can witness to. I knew that what I had in Jesus, my infant son had also.

When had this happened to Doug? We had brought him to the Lord in baptism. He had been the object of prayers for a long time. Was it through the faith of his mother? Did this happen to him when it happened to me as I opened my heart?

I do not know, but one thing I know. My son Doug had a heart trust in the Lord even as I had. And Doug learned to pray and call upon the Lord from the time he learned to talk. And he is a Christian today. He always has been a good and godly son. He cannot look back to the time of his conversion. His witness is, "I have been a Christian for as long as I can remember." That is the way it should be in the household of faith.

Discussion
1. If a child can have saving faith and thereby become a disciple, when should that child be baptized?
2. What constitutes "a household of faith?"
3. Why did God ask Abraham to circumcise male children (Genesis 17:4-9)? How would a child break this covenant according to verse 9? Does this have any application to the present age?
4. Were all circumcised Hebrews saved? Are all baptized people saved today? Why or why not?
5. What scriptural backing is there for baptizing children of a believing parent?
6. If Jesus linked belief and baptism, "make disciples and baptize" and "he who believes and is baptized shall be saved," how can we know if a little child has faith?
7. What should we tell our children as to the meaning of their baptism?

7

The modes of baptism

"I will sprinkle *clean water upon you, and you shall be clean from all your uncleannesses, and from all your idols I will cleanse you. A new heart I will give you, and a new spirit I will put within you; and I will take out of your flesh the heart of stone and give you a heart of flesh. And I will put my spirit within you, and cause you to walk in my statutes and be careful to observe my ordinances" (Ezekiel 36:25-27 RSV).*

"Let us draw near with a true heart in full assurance of faith, with our hearts sprinkled clean *from an evil conscience and our bodies washed with pure water" (Hebrews 10:22 RSV).*

"And such were some of you. But you were washed, *you were sanctified, you were justified in the name of the Lord Jesus Christ and in the Spirit of our God" (I Corinthians 6:11 RSV).*

"And now why do you wait? Rise and be baptized, and wash *away your sins, calling on His name" (Acts 22:16 RSV).*

"Husbands, love your wives, as Christ loved the Church and gave himself for her, that he might sanctify her, having cleansed her by the washing of water with the word" *(Ephesians 5:25 RSV).*

*"Do you not know that all of us who have been bap-
tized into Christ Jesus were baptized into his death: we
were buried therefore with him by baptism into death,
so that as Christ was raised from the dead by the glory
of the Father, we too might walk in newness of life"
(Romans 6:3-4 RSV).*

*"And you were buried with him in baptism, in which
you were also raised with him through faith in the working of God who raised him from the dead" (Colossians
2:12 RSV).*

For hundreds of years, three major modes of baptism
have been used in the Christian Church: washing,
sprinkling and immersion. Despite efforts to unify baptismal practices within the body of Christ, the Church
still uses the three modes. Observing the results does not
show any mode of baptism to be superior to another.
Spurgeon was an immersionist; Wesley sprinkled;
Luther washed. But the Lord used all three men mightily in their time to bring the Gospel of salvation to the
sons of men.

The Greek word *baptizo* has been translated quite
uniformly into the English language as baptize, but one
cannot be dogmatic as to what this word actually
means. Young in his *Analytical Concordance to the Bible* gives that word the meaning, "to consecrate by
pouring water out on, or putting into." Thus he affirms
all modes from the very root meaning of the word.
Various theologians have written very convincingly
about all three modes of baptism and become rather
dogmatic about the correctness of their own interpretation and its Biblical backing.

This same root word *baptizo* is used in Mark 7 where
it speaks of washing *(baptismos)* the hands, cups, pots,
vessels of bronze and beds. From its use in that one

sentence one can see support for the argument that immersion is not the only meaning of that word. In secular writings by authors living during the time of the apostles, the same word was used in respect to washing furniture, houses and other objects that could not possibly be immersed. However, hands, pots, cups and the like could be immersed.

Space will not permit a theological treatise on the subject, but I will point out the Biblical background for each of the three modes. The reader may draw his own conclusion.

The mode of *sprinkling* has been used by many denominations for hundreds of years. Water is sprinkled upon the forehead, either from the hand, or a branch, or a rose; this is done three times in the name of the triune God.

The prophet Ezekiel received a prophetic word from the Lord in which he was told what to expect under the New Covenant: "I will take you from the nations, and gather you from all countries, and bring you into your own land. I will *sprinkle clean water* upon you, and you shall be clean from all your uncleannesses, and from all your idols I will cleanse you. A new heart will I give you, and a new spirit I will put within you; and I will take out of your flesh the heart of stone and give you a heart of flesh" (36:24-26). The proponents of baptism by sprinkling point to this verse which obviously speaks of salvation under the New Covenant after the coming of Christ.

For the ceremonial cleansing of the altar, Book (Scriptures), and people of Israel, the Lord commanded Moses to take the blood of the sin offering and mix it with water. Then he dipped hyssop (a branch from a tree) into the basin containing the water and the blood and sprinkled the altar, the Book and the people. We read: "And Moses took the blood (mixed with water) and threw it upon the people and said, 'Behold the blood of the covenant which the Lord has made with you in accordance with these words' " (Exodus 24:6-8). This was done to bring them into the covenant of blood, to give them a judicial cleansing, and to purify them through the sacrifice of an innocent substitute, the clean animal.

The writer of the book of Hebrews refers to this sprinkling of the altar, Book and people of Israel by saying, "Moses took the blood of calves and goats, with *water* and scarlet wool and hyssop, and *sprinkled* both the book itself and the people, saying, 'This is the blood of the covenant which God commanded you' . . . indeed, under the law almost everything is purified with blood, and without the shedding of blood there is no forgiveness" (Hebrews 9:19-22).

Then the same chapter says, "For if the *sprinkling* of defiled persons with the blood of goats and bulls and with the ashes of a heifer sanctifies for the purification of the flesh, how much more shall the blood of Christ, who through the eternal Spirit offered himself without blemish to God, purify your conscience from dead works to serve the living God" (Hebrews 9:13,14). The proponents of sprinkling see the act of Moses as symbolic of water baptism, which unites the believer with the death of Christ, and hence symbolic of His blood which purifies the conscience.

The Levitical priests were cleansed individually by having "the water of expiation sprinkled over them" (Numbers 8:7). This was done in much the same way as Moses purified the people, for the sin offering was blood mixed with water, thus making it "the water of expiation." Under the New Covenant all Christians are priests (I Peter 2:5,9) and are individually cleansed by "the waters of expiation" (baptism), having their "hearts *sprinkled* clean from an evil conscience and their bodies washed with pure water," as the writer of Hebrews says in 10:22.

Some proponents of sprinkling surmise that John the Baptist baptized by sprinkling. John was the son of Zechariah, a priest, and had witnessed his father practicing ceremonial sprinkling perhaps hundreds of times. The priests used the hyssop with scarlet wool dipped in water or the waters of expiation, and sprinkled unclean people to cleanse them.

We who are in the Kingdom of God have come to "Jesus, the mediator of a New Covenant, and to the *sprinkled* blood that speaks more graciously than the blood of Abel" (Hebrews 12:24). The proponents of baptism by sprinkling believe the blood of Christ is involved in their baptism into Christ, and make a rather strong case from the Scriptures in this regard. Therefore, it behooves anyone with different convictions to avoid ridicule, which has been rather flagrant among the different exponents of water baptism, and to refrain from dogmatic assertions.

Now let us take a look at the case for baptism by *washing*.

In the church where I came to Christ, the pastor used washing for baptism, dipping his hand into the baptismal font and taking a generous handful of water to apply to the forehead of the person being baptized. This was done three times, once for each person of the Trinity. It was the only mode that I knew for several years. And when I was in the parish ministry, I baptized in the same way.

Those who think the correct mode is washing point to the words of Josephus, a historian living at the time of John, who speaks of John's baptism as a "washing."

While a blinded Saul of Tarsus was waiting in the city of Damascus, God gave him a vision, telling him that a man named Ananias would come to him. At the same time the Lord sent Ananias to Saul. After the two came together, Ananias laid hands on Saul saying, "Saul, receive your sight." In that very hour his sight returned. Then Ananias said, "The God of our fathers appointed you to know his will, to see the Just One (Jesus) and to hear a voice from his mouth; for you will be a witness for him to all men of what you have seen and heard. And now why do you wait? Rise and be baptized and *wash* away your sins, calling on his name" (Acts 9:22). The proponents of baptizing by washing see that word *wash* and believe that the inner washing away of sin corresponds to the outer mode of baptism, that is, washing.

The Apostle Paul, in speaking to Christians who once lived immoral and ungodly lives, wrote, "But you were *washed,* you were sanctified, you were justified in the name of the Lord Jesus Christ and in the Spirit of our God" (I Corinthians 6:11). Some Christians feel that this verse implies the mode of washing, even though the verse does not refer directly to the mode, but speaks primarily of that inner washing of the spirit of a man.

David wrote, "Purge me with hyssop, and I shall be clean; *wash* me, and I shall be whiter than snow." David clearly intimates that his inner washing came as a consequence of the outer application of water, either with the hyssop by sprinkling, or by washing, the two common modes used by the priests.

Paul writes of the love of Jesus Christ for the Church and how He "gave himself up for her, that he might sanctify her, having cleansed her by the *washing of water with the word*" (Ephesians 5:25).

In Hebrews 10:22 believers are encouraged to draw near to the throne of grace and are reminded that they have had their "bodies *washed with pure water.*" In the book of Titus are the words, "He saved us, not by works which we have done in righteousness, but in virtue of his own mercy, by the *washing of regeneration* and renewal in the Holy Spirit, which he poured out upon us richly through Jesus Christ, our Savior" (3:5). Admittedly, these are not clear directives to the mode of baptism, but they are suggestive.

As there were ceremonial sprinklings for cleansing in the Old Testament, so there were all manner of ceremonial washings—washings of vessels used in temple worship, clothing worn by priests, the bodies of the priests, unclean persons. The washings were as common as the sprinklings, and had the same connotation of judicial cleansing.

The proponents for washing in baptism do not quarrel with those who sprinkle and generally consider the mode immaterial. They look to the long historical record of baptism by washing in the Roman Catholic Church, practiced for over a thousand years before the reformers came on the scene and the Anabaptists began baptism by immersion. They recognize baptisms by immersion but believe the amount of water has nothing to do with the effectiveness of this ordinance. They look to Luther who said that baptism is by water with the Word and, therefore, the amount of water used is immaterial. Peter said that baptism was not "the washing away of the filth of the flesh" (I Peter 3:21) and, therefore, immersion seems unnecessary to those who baptize by washing.

True, among the advocates of sprinkling and washing have arisen many sacramentalists, that is, people who believe that God works regeneration regardless of the heart condition of the person baptized. However, many others look at baptism as Luther did—saying it requires a subjective condition called faith for baptism to be effective. These individuals work in their respective fields to so preach and teach the Word that faith will be created in the hearts of those to whom they minister.

The large contingent in Christendom who believe in baptism by immersion look to the word *baptizo,* which in the Greek language means to "dip" or to "immerse." They hold that this is the main meaning of the word. They are equally convinced that John the Baptist used immersion. The statement about the baptism of Jesus, "And when he came up out of the water," implies to this group of Christians that Jesus was immersed.

As the proponents of sprinkling and washing look to Roman Catholic tradition for the basis of their baptismal practices, immersionists look to the two-thousand-year old Eastern Orthodox tradition of baptizing by immersion. And some Baptists claim that the Roman Catholic Church changed its mode of baptism from immersion to washing in 1311.

Immersionists look to Romans 6 where Paul writes: "Do not you know that all of us who have been baptized into Christ have been baptized into his death? We were *buried* therefore with him by baptism into death" (v. 4). To the immersionist the word *buried* obviously indicates, that baptism should be by immersion. The same truth is reiterated in Colossians 2, "And you were buried with him in baptism, in which you were also raised with him through faith" (v. 12). The only way one can be buried in baptism is to be immersed. Immersionists point to the words of Luther which declare that immersion is to be desired because of the symbolism involved.

These Christians say that all the Scripture which speaks about being washed perfectly fits immersion also. And this is true.

The symbolism of baptism by immersion is meaningful and descriptive. By his baptism the person dies to his former way of life and all it stood for. He enters into Christ's death. Then he arises from his baptism together with Christ to walk in newness of life. This fits in beautifully with Romans 6 and Colossians 2.

There is a strong case for baptism by immersion. Those who practice immersion have strong convictions and believe implicitly that this is the only mode of baptism which fits the meaning of Scripture. They often upset the faith of other Christians by saying rather pointedly that those who have been sprinkled or washed have not been baptized at all.

Discussion

1. Does the meaning and usage of the Greek word *baptizo* give more support to one mode of baptism than to the others?

2. Is the word of the Lord to Ezekiel, "I will sprinkle clean water upon you," a reference to water baptism or to spiritual cleansing? Could it be both?

3. Do you think the writer of Hebrews refers to baptism when he writes "and to the sprinkled blood" in Hebrews 12:24?

4. Are the Old Testament ceremonial cleansings typological of New Testament baptism?

5. Does the symbolism of spiritual death and resurrection apply only to baptism by immersion?

6. Will God honor convictions thought to be based upon His Word even though the convictions are erroneous?

7. Why does your church use its mode of baptism?

8

Is the mode of baptism specified?

"John answered them, 'I baptize with water. . .'"
(John 1:26 RSV).
"So those who received his word were baptized"
(Acts 2:41 RSV).
"They were baptized" (Acts 8:12 RSV).
"And he baptized him" (Acts 8:38 RSV).
"Then he rose and was baptized" (Acts 9:18 RSV).
"And he commanded them to be baptized" (Acts
10:48 RSV).
"When she was baptized" (Acts 16:15 RSV).
"And he was baptized at once, with all his family"
(Acts 16:33 RSV).
"And many of the Corinthians hearing Paul believed
and were baptized" (Acts 18:8 RSV).
"They were baptized in the name of the Lord Jesus"
(Acts 19:5 RSV).
"Rise and be baptized" (Acts 22:16 RSV).

Let us carefully examine the words of Scripture telling how John baptized. How did he baptize Jesus?

In Matthew's Gospel the record says: "And when
Jesus was baptized, he went up immediately from the
water, and behold, the heavens were opened" (3:16).

The record in Mark: "And Jesus was baptized of
John. And when he came up out of the water, immediately he saw the heavens opened" (1:9).

61

The record in Luke: "And when Jesus also had been baptized and was praying, the heaven opened" (3:21).

As I have already said, many hold that John the Baptist baptized with the hyssop, for that was the ceremonial way of cleansing for the Israelites. But nothing in the above words would substantiate baptism either by sprinkling or by immersion. One's background easily influences what he reads in these three accounts.

Some visualize John and Jesus in the water with John stooping to dip water up by his hand, and Jesus bending over to receive that washing over His head. Others will visualize John with the hyssop, dipping it into the water and sprinkling Jesus as they did in the Old Testament. Others will see Jesus and John waist deep in the water as John immerses Jesus. And each picture will fit into what has been written about the baptism of Jesus.

How did John baptize? He said, "I baptize with water" (John 1:26,31,33). For a time he baptized "beyond the Jordan" (John 1:28), "in the Jordan" (Mark 1:9); and he also baptized at Aenon, near Salim "because there was much water there" (John 3:23). John could have baptized by immersion in the River Jordan, but in Aenon today there are only seven small springs, no lake or river. Immersion could have been a problem there. In Bethany beyond Jordan where he also baptized, there is no body of water. Again it would have been difficult there to baptize by immersion. Nothing can be proved by the places where John baptized as to the mode of baptism he used, but immersion seems unlikely in some of them.

But let us look at the record in respect to others who were baptized. On the day of Pentecost after Peter had preached his sermon, he said, "So those who received the Word were baptized" (Acts 2:41). How? Nothing said. But 3,000 people were baptized that day and it seemed to create no problem. We know how difficult it would be to baptize 3,000 people today with no baptistry, lake or river available. However, if the disciples used sprinkling or washing, they could have done it easily.

I recall the testimony of a general from Generalissimo Chiang Kai-shek's army. He was a lay preacher and spoke at Luther Seminary while I was a student. He said that during the war, as they were seeking to defend against the Communist invasion, he preached a sermon to an entire regiment of soldiers. Several thousand of them responded to his Gospel call.

He said that there was no time for individual baptisms. The Communists were attacking and the defenders were in imminent danger. Therefore, he took a water hose and baptized them all at the same time in "the name of the Father, the Son, and the Holy Ghost." And his concluding remark: "You cannot tell me that they were not baptized. That afternoon the Communists made their attack and over half of those soldiers who had been baptized were killed. I know they all went home to be with the Lord, and that took the sting out of an otherwise calamitous day."

Philip was used mightily of the Lord in healing, working miracles and reaching Samaritans for salvation in Jesus Christ. "And when they believed Philip as he preached good news about the kingdom of God and the name of Jesus Christ, they were baptized, both men and women. And even Simon himself believed and after being baptized continued with Philip" (Acts 8:12,13). Nothing is said about the mode of baptism.

Philip baptized the Ethiopian treasurer on the way to Gaza. "They both went down into the water and he baptized him" (Acts 8:26-39). Today there is one small spring of water in Gaza. There are no lakes or rivers. But whatever that situation, nothing is said about how

Philip baptized. They both went into the water and they both came up out of the water. Nothing is said of the mode, only implied.

In respect to Saul's baptism: "Then he rose and was baptized." With Cornelius and his household: "And he commanded them to be baptized." With Lydia: "And when she was baptized with her household." The Philippian jailer: "And he was baptized with all his family." The Corinthians: "And many of the Corinthians hearing Paul believed and were baptized." The Ephesians: "They were baptized in the name of the Lord Jesus Christ." There are no specifics as to the mode, and there are no definitive answers to our question.

The word *baptizo,* which is translated in English, "baptize," does mean to "dip" and to "immerse," but it also means to "pour water out upon," as we have indicated before.

What is the evidence historically in respect to the mode of baptism? The oldest record is found in *Antiquities of the Jews,* Book XVIII, page 540, by Josephus, a historian writing at the time of John the Baptist.

Now some of the Jews thought that the destruction of Herod's army came from God, and that very justly, as a punishment of what he did against John, that was called the Baptist; for Herod slew him, who was a good man, and commanded the Jews to exercise virtue, both as to righteousness towards God, and so to come to baptism; for that washing with water would be acceptable to him, if they made use of it, not in order to the putting away of the remission of some sins only, but for the purification of the body; supposing still that soul was thoroughly purified beforehand by righteousness.

The Roman Catholics maintain that they have consistently baptized the infants of the members and adult converts by sprinkling or washing since apostolic days. Their records reveal that they followed the ritual of baptism developed by Gregory the Great, A.D. 590-604, all through the middle ages and following. That method was to apply water upon the head three times in the name of the Father, the Son and the Holy Ghost. This was also the tradition of the Thomists of India, some two million in number today, who trace their foundations to the Apostle Thomas.

However, the Eastern Orthodox Churches immerse their children by dipping them under the water three times, once for the Father, for the Son and for the Holy Ghost. In speaking with a historian of this denomination, I was told that their records trace this practice all the way back to the early church fathers. When I asked this historian about the baptism of adults, I learned that in their large cathedral in St. Paul, Minnesota, they had no baptistry large enough for an adult. Their practice was to baptize adults by washing. I was told that this practice for adults was quite general.

The Lutherans, Methodists, Episcopalians, Presbyterians, and their offshoots, have sprinkled and washed throughout their history. The oldest of these denominations goes back a little over 350 years. But the Baptists, Mission Covenant, Plymouth Brethren, most Pentecostal churches, and the hundreds of offshoot congregations and denominations have practiced baptism by immersion, beginning with the Anabaptists during the Reformation. There are exceptions. Among the Pentecostal churches is the large and growing Methodist Pentecostal Church of Chile with 700,000 members today. They still baptize their infants with sprinkling, as they did before breaking away from the Methodist church in that country.

Many new congregations have sprung up in the past few years due to the outpouring of the Holy Spirit and the advent again of charismatic gifts and power. Not a few of these have had difficulties in deciding what baptismal practice to follow. Many congregations have opened the door to all modes of baptism, leaving the time and mode to the discretion of the parents, or the individual when he or she is an adult.

Why has there been such a dearth of clear and cogent evidence on this matter? The Lord knew in His omniscience that this problem would arise in His Church and could have obviated the confusion by giving one clear statement on the *how* of baptism. But there is none. Apparently, there is a lesson for all of us to learn. We are called to love and accept one another, even though we have doctrinal differences.

It is apparent that there is Scriptural backing for all three modes of baptism. It is also apparent that the advocates of each mode are convinced that what they are doing is based upon the Word of God. The Holy Spirit has worked salvation in all three camps, and baptismal modes seem to present no handicap in either of the three camps in reaching souls for Jesus Christ.

I have noted too, as one who has been used in ecumenical meetings where people have sought the anointing of the Holy Spirit, that the Holy Spirit has fallen upon people irrespective of their particular mode of baptism. Yet Peter said on the day of Pentecost that repentance and baptism were conditions for the reception of the gift of the Holy Spirit.

Historically, there have been revivals in nearly all denominations irrespective of their distinctive doctrine on baptism. This is true of those who have baptized their children, including infants; and it is true of those who have waited to baptize their children until they either make a decision of faith in Christ or reach the age of accountability. It is obvious that pastors and parents have been convinced that the teaching of their own denomination on baptism has been correct, and the Holy Spirit has honored them. We should honor one another's convictions.

Discussion
1. How do preconceived ideas influence people's interpretations of Scripture?
2. Is baptism simply by water with the Word, irrespective of the amount of water used?
3. Does the history of the Christian Church prove that baptism was by immersion? Are the millions who have been baptized by sprinkling or washing, in fact, not baptized, as some say?
4. With the very precise instructions given by the Lord to Moses for purification under the ceremonial law, why wasn't the Lord just as precise in respect to the mode of baptism?
5. What does this lack of guidance say to you about how strongly one should hold to convictions in this area?

9

A call to charity

"*Remind them of this, and charge them before the Lord to avoid disputing about words, which does no good, but only ruins the hearers*" (II Timothy 2:14 RSV).

"*As for the man who is weak in faith, welcome him, but not for disputes over opinions. One believes he may eat anything, while the weak man eats only vegetables. Let not him who eats despise him who abstains, and let not him who abstains pass judgment on him who eats; for God has welcomed him. Who are you to pass judgment on the servant of another? It is before his own master that he stands or falls. And he will be upheld, for the Master is able to make him stand*" (Romans 14:1-4 RSV).

"*I do not pray for these only, but also for those who believe in me through their word, that they may all be one; even as thou, Father, art in me, and I in thee, that they also may be in us, so that the world may believe that thou hast sent me*" (John 17:20-21 RSV).

"*Awake, and strengthen what remains and is on the point of death, for I have not found your works perfect in the sight of my God. Remember then what you received and heard; keep that, and* repent. *If you will*

68

*not awake, I will come like a thief, and you will not
know at what hour I will come upon you" (Revelation
3:2,3 RSV).*

Because of the present move of the Holy Spirit
throughout the world, many large ecumenical con-
ferences are being held. Those attending come from
many different backgrounds, representing many different beliefs and practices concerning water baptism.

Many who have found a meaningful faith in Christ,
and, perhaps, have gone on to receive the anointing
power of the Holy Spirit, have become troubled over
their baptism in their own church. When a person has
come from a congregation where spiritual life is at a low
ebb and then finds an assured faith and experiences the
baptism of the Holy Spirit, any attack upon the
theology of his own denomination and its practices on
baptism may meet with his approval. Especially when
the person was baptized as an infant or an adult without
a heart trust in the Lord, he may suspect the theology
and the practices of his own church in that particular.

I recall a few years back being called into a home
fellowship in St. Paul, Minnesota, where the question
of rebaptism was posed. It was a Lutheran women's Bible study group. Several of them had been to a spiritual
retreat and had received the anointing of the Holy Spirit
and spoke in tongues. Thereafter they had been ap-
proached about being rebaptized. They were told that
their baptism as infants in the Lutheran church was not
valid and were exhorted "to follow the Lord Jesus
Christ into the baptismal waters," which to their
counselors meant immersion. These women were con-
fused and had been searching the Scriptures, wondering
what to do.

After some discussion I told them that the condition
for receiving the anointing of the Holy Spirit was a true

faith in Jesus Christ and a baptism into His name for the remission of sins. Since the Holy Spirit had come upon them with gifts, God had recognized the authenticity of their baptism. I asked them, "Why then don't you recognize your baptism too?" This was good news to them and settled the matter immediately.

Today a host of people have been rebaptized, believing that their previous baptism was invalid for one reason or another. They may doubt the spirituality of the pastor who performed their baptism or consider his theology of baptism unscriptural. Does the character, spirituality or theology of a pastor vitiate baptism?

I think of an actual case where the pastor had been immoral and heretical, and he had baptized people over a period of fifteen years. Were all his baptismal acts void? With a new pastor, this congregation said no.

The church has had to deal with the problems posed by the faith and morals of an officiant at baptisms, marriages and other Christian rites and has uniformly held that these acts are perfectly valid before the Lord. The person involved can rest upon the spiritual authority vested in that pastor and need not question his character or faith.

I recall leading a soldier to Christ. He repented and called upon the Lord for forgiveness, inviting Jesus Christ into his life. The following Sunday evening he was baptized. Two weeks later, however, he came to my office to relate the tremendous conversion experience he had one week after his baptism! Then came the question: "Do I have to be rebaptized?" I assured him that his baptism was valid, even though he had this experience after the fact. I know the same thing has happened with pastors in other denominations. Generally speaking, there have been no rebaptisms in such cases.

If a Christian leaves his church and goes back to his old life, then later repents and experiences the grace of

God, we do not require him to be rebaptized. Who is to judge whether he had completely fallen away or what really happened in his valley experience? If rebaptism were the order for such a case, it would be the order for almost every Christian, for all go through valley experiences of one kind or another. And this may occur even though one maintains regular church attendance.

We have seen from the Scriptures that the entire nation of Israel was in covenant relationship with God through circumcision. However, both the prophets and the apostles maintained that only a remnant truly believed; that is, only a small fraction of the entire congregation of Israel were right with God (Isaiah 10:22; Hosea 1:10; Romans 9:6-8,27; 11:5). If a Jew did not truly believe, his circumcision became uncircumcision, the Apostle Paul said (Romans 2:25). And the call to the Jew from the Old Testament was not to be recircumcised (if he were a male) but to return to the Lord (Isaiah 55:6).

Baptism, like circumcision, involves a covenant relationship with God. The covenant in baptism could be spelled out in this manner: God promises to be your Father, Jesus Christ your Redeemer, and the Holy Spirit your Sanctifier, on the condition that you believe in Jesus Christ. As circumcision was a once-for-all transaction, so baptism should be a once-for-all transaction. And as a heart faith in the Lord was the condition which validated circumcision, so a heart faith in the Lord is the condition which validates baptism.

There are many warnings in the Scriptures about Christians falling away from God. In the book of Hebrews are four major warnings about falling away (Hebrews 2:1-4, 3:12-19, 6:4-9, 10:26-39). The writer exhorts Christians to believe the Word and draw near to the Lord, but does not even intimate that they should be rebaptized.

71

Again in the message which Jesus Christ gave John for His seven churches in Asia Minor are warnings about falling away, about some whose garments were already spotted, some who were lukewarm. But the exhortations to them are not to be rebaptized, but rather to repent, to remember what they had received and heard, to open their hearts to the Lord and thus be renewed and made alive in Christ.

When a person is told, or believes from the Scriptures, that his baptism is ineffectual, who can blame that person for submitting to rebaptism? However, it is upsetting to a pastor and his members when one of their own has gone elsewhere and has submitted to another baptism and comes home to his congregation with this testimony. This rebaptism says to that congregation that they are in error in their way of baptizing.

Rebaptism is understandable when a person leaves one fellowship to join another congregation where a different mode is practiced. Or where a person has been a lapsed member of one congregation and then is converted in another and is asked to receive baptism. But where a person still belongs to a congregation and then is rebaptized by another, what he does implies repudiation of what his own congregation is doing. This has caused real conflict and heartaches.

I recall rebaptizing a woman who had first been baptized as a Roman Catholic. Later she joined a Baptist church and was immersed. Then she married a Mormon and joined that church, but had to be rebaptized by them according to their tradition. Later both she and her husband began attending regularly in our congregation, and there she had her first experience of a true repentance and conversion.

She came to me asking to be baptized again. After hearing her story, I told her she did not need a further baptism. However, she explained that when she was baptized as a Mormon, she was asked to renounce all previous religious knowledge and experience, including her baptisms in the Catholic and Baptist churches. Because of these circumstances and to quiet her conscience, I did baptize this woman in accord with her desire. She testified to a peace of mind thereafter. I am convinced this situation was a proper time for rebaptism.

Now that the Holy Spirit is falling upon people of all denominations irrespective of their teaching on baptism, and we see congregations coming into life and power with God in all denominations, it is apparent that God is not as concerned about the time and mode of baptism as we are. This is a call to all for charity, that the unity Christ desires for His church may come, in spite of doctrinal differences and ritual variations. When one sees the gifts of the Spirit in operation with all manner of healings and miracles, in churches of many denominations including the Roman Catholics, it is clear that God can work mightily wherever there is faith in His Word, life in His people, and an openness to receive all that belongs in the Kingdom, in spite of the particular teaching in the matter of baptism.

Churches must set aside a false trust in baptism. Souls are not saved because they have been baptized, any more than a Jew was saved because he had been circumcised. If you baptize an unconverted, unrepentant adult, he will not be changed into a believer in Christ by baptism. And likewise, when you baptize children who are not in the household of faith, apart from those who come to faith on their own, the children will still be "unclean" as Paul wrote in I Corinthians 7:14.

The evangelical fathers of nearly all denominations have quite consistently held that baptism does not work *ex opere operato,* that is, as a mechanical operation having an efficacy without faith. But when churches lose their spiritual vitality, their practices often deny their own beliefs. A crass sacramentalism can take hold of such people and a false assurance can unconsciously develop—an assurance that is contrary even to the confession of that church.

Christians need to develop charity and sympathetic understanding for other believers. Paul said that some Christians are unlearned in some things, such as the eating of meats offered to idols. He says that eating such meat will not defile one who is enlightened, and he has freedom to eat. However, someone who eats such meat against his conscience will defile himself. Others who have enlightenment on the matter must respect the unenlightened person, and even refrain from using his liberty to eat, so that he will not cause a weaker brother to stumble (I Corinthians 8:7-13).

While I was in parish ministry, I learned to love and work together with ministers of various denominations. We met once a week to pray not only for each other and for our respective ministries, but also for the field of endeavor where we had a common interest.

One of the Baptist ministers, the Reverend Cully Olson, became a very close friend. We ate at each other's homes on occasions. He had two daughters and I had two sons. I recall how we prayed all around, including the children. When I heard his little ones pray, they moved my heart by their sincere faith. There was no difference between his children and mine. But ours were baptized and his were not. However, his children were to be baptized when they made their independent decisions for Christ.

I learned to respect his understanding as he learned to respect mine. This pastor believed in water baptism even as I did, but we had different understandings in the matter. If he were unenlightened, or if I were unenlightened, we both had to respect each other's convictions and conscience, and so we did. He was convinced from the Scriptures and I was convinced from the Scriptures. We both agreed that the Scriptures contained the truth, if we could but see it.

When we have faith in Jesus Christ, the Father places Christ in us and us in Christ. We then have become partakers of the divine nature. We are sons of God through faith in Jesus Christ. And then we can take comfort that we through baptism, however done, were united to Him, to His death, to His burial, to His resurrection. By faith our baptism is consummated and has become effectual.

Then as we look across to other vineyards of the Lord's planting, we need not look for words and doctrine which are in accord exactly with our own, but we look for "fruit." "By their fruit ye shall know them," as our Lord said so aptly. We know from the Word that the fruit of the Spirit—love, joy, peace, patience and all the rest—can only come through an abiding faith in Jesus Christ. If we see fruit, even though there may be differences in practice and doctrine, we know that the Lord is there, that these are His children, our brothers and sisters in Christ with whom we are joined in the Spirit. We owe them one thing, *to love them.*

Discussion
1. Under what circumstances should a Christian be rebaptized?
2. Are there distinct advantages for the Christian who has been immersed?
3. What is the safest criterion to use to determine whether or not a person is really a Christian?
4. How important is unity of doctrine to the unity of the Spirit in the body of Christ? What constitutes the unity of the Spirit?

5. Do you find it difficult to love those who differ with you in doctrine? In what practical ways might love in this case be developed and expressed?

APPENDIX

For your guidance and further consideration of the important subject of water baptism, two additions to the body of this book follow.

1. Statements from the major main-line Protestant denominations describing water baptism as practiced in their churches or fellowships.

2. A listing, for the most part chronological, of references in the New Testament concerning water baptism.

We believe a reading of both of these sections will prove both enlightening and helpful to your consideration of this subject.

Assemblies of God
(The Assemblies of God)

The ordinance of baptism by immersion is commanded in the Scriptures. All who repent and believe on Christ as Saviour and Lord are to be baptized. Thus they declare to the world that they have died with Christ and that they also have been raised with Him to walk in newness of life (Matthew 28:19; Mark 16:16; Acts 10:47,48; Romans 6:4).

—General Council Constitution, Article V
The General Council of the Assemblies of God

Baptists
(Southern Baptist Convention)

IV. THE CHURCH
3. Its Ordinances
Baptism and the Lord's Supper are the two ordinances of the church. They are symbolic, but their observance involves faith, confession, self-examination, discernment, gratitude, dedication, fellowship, and worship. Baptism is to be administered by the church under the authority of the triune God and is the immersion in water of those who by faith have received Jesus as Saviour and Lord. In that act the believer is portrayed as buried with Christ and raised with him to walk in newness of life.

The Lord's Supper, observed through the symbols of the bread and the cup, is a sober searching of one's heart, a thankful remembrance of Christ and his sacrificial death on the cross, a blessed assurance of his return, and a joyous fellowship with the living Christ and his people.

Baptism and the Lord's Supper, the two ordinances of the church, are symbolic of redemption, but their observance involves spiritual realities in personal Christian experience.

—*Baptist Ideals,* The Sunday School Board
of the Southern Baptist Church

Evangelical Friends Church

58. When Jesus had His last supper with His disciples
    He made statements which have at times been inter-
    preted (1) as calling for a perpetual new testament
    observance or (2) as a new meaning for the Passover
    meal which they were partaking of together. The
    unleavened bread was to represent His body about
    to be broken for them and the wine, the blood which
    He was about to shed. The early church and most
    Christians to this day have taken the first interpre-
    tation.
59. Friends, impressed with the abuses which had grown
    up about this observance and the use of water in
    Christian baptism, and which substituted the out-
    ward for the inner spiritual reality—an abuse which
    persists to this day—placed their emphasis upon the
    spiritual content and let the outward symbols fall in-
    to disuse. But in 1886 this Yearly Meeting felt con-
    strained to grant liberty concerning the use or non-
    use of the outward elements of bread and wine in
    communion and of water in Christian baptism, while
    cautioning against any failure to achieve real spiri-
    tual sharing in the death of Christ and in the baptism
    of the Holy Spirit. We caution also against the too
    frequent use of the symbols lest familiarity breed
    contempt.
60. Each of our congregations may arrange services—
    perhaps in special meetings rather than in the regular
    worship services, in order to treat tenderly the con-
    sciences of those who protest the use of outward sym-
    bols—for baptism and communion upon the request

of members. If a pastor feels a conviction against administering the ordinances, he may enlist the services of a fellow pastor in the observance. In all such services it should be abundantly clear to all the congregation that Friends have the right to abstain from as well as to participate in the observance. In these services it should also be clear that the observances are only symbols of an inward spiritual experience.

—Faith and Practice
The Book of Discipline
Evangelical Friends Church

Episcopal
(Protestant Episcopal Church in the U.S.A.)

A Catechism

QUESTION: What is your Name?
Answer: N. or N.N.
Question: Who gave you this Name?
Answer: My Sponsors in Baptism; wherein I was made a member of Christ, the child of God, and an inheritor of the kingdom of heaven.
Question: What did your Sponsors then for you?
Answer: They did promise and vow three things in my name: First, that I should renounce the devil and all his works, the pomps and vanity of this wicked world, and all the sinful lusts of the flesh; Secondly, that I should believe all the Articles of the Christian Faith; And Thirdly, that I should keep God's holy will and commandments, and walk in the same all the days of my life.
Question: How many Sacraments hath Christ ordained in his Church?
Answer: Two only, as generally necessary to salvation; that is to say, Baptism, and the Supper of the Lord.
Question: What meanest thou by this word *Sacrament?*
Answer: I mean an outward and visible sign of an inward and spiritual grace given unto us; ordained by Christ himself, as a means whereby we receive the same, and a pledge to assure us thereof.
Question: How many parts are there in a Sacrament?
Answer: Two; the outward visible sign, and the inward spiritual grace.
Question: What is the outward visible sign or form in Baptism?

Answer: Water; wherein the person is baptized, In the Name of the Father, and of the Son, and of the Holy Ghost.

Question: What is the inward and spiritual grace?

Answer: A death unto sin, and a new birth unto righteousness: for being by nature born in sin, and the children of wrath, we are hereby made the children of grace.

Question: What is required of persons to be baptized?

Answer: Repentance, whereby they forsake sin; and Faith, whereby they stedfastly believe the promises of God made to them in that Sacrament.

Question: Why then are Infants baptized, when by reason of their tender age they cannot perform them?

Answer: Because they promise them both by their Sureties; which promise, when they come to age, themselves are bound to perform.

—The Book of Common Prayer
and Administration of the Sacraments
and Other Rites and Ceremonies of the Church
Protestant Episcopal Church in the U.S.A.

Lutheran
(Lutheran Council in the U.S.A.)

IX. BAPTISM (German)

It is taught among us that Baptism is necessary and that grace is offered through it. Children, too, should be baptized, for in Baptism they are committed to God and become acceptable to him.

On this account the Anabaptists who teach that infant Baptism is not right are rejècted.

IX. BAPTISM (Latin)

Our churches teach that Baptism is necessary for salvation, that the grace of God is offered through Baptism, and that children should be baptized, for being offered to God through Baptism they are received into his grace.

Our churches condemn the Anabaptists who reject the Baptism of children and declare that children are saved without Baptism.

—The Book of Concord, The Confessions of the Evangelical Lutheran Church, Fortress Press.

The Reformed Church in America

THE ORDER FOR THE BAPTISM OF ADULTS
AND THEIR
ADMISSION TO THE LORD'S TABLE

The Constitution of The Reformed Church in America (Article 6) states that it is the office of the elders together with the minister of the Word to ". . .pass upon the fitness of those who desire to make public confession of faith. . ." (Sec. 1c). "Only those persons may be received as members of the Church in full communion who have made confession of their faith in the Lord Jesus Christ before the Board of Elders. . ." (Sec. 6a). From this it seems clear that the minister, if any, and elders shall pass on the fitness of persons desiring to be baptized and received into full communion, admit such as are found to be properly prepared, and authorize their reception into full membership and admission to the Lord's Table before the congregation.

The following procedure and office fulfill these constitutional provisions. The Order consists of two parts, the one before the elders, offered as a suggestion, and the one before the congregation.

BEFORE THE ELDERS

The suggested Order for the interrogation is the same as that for those baptized in infancy seeking admission to holy Communion. It is given in the following Order, which see.

BEFORE THE CONGREGATION

Baptism and admission to holy Communion should be before the congregation. As one of the Sacraments, Baptism should be administered after the service of the Word. See the outline for the sequence.

THE ORDER FOR THE SACRAMENT
OF
INFANT BAPTISM

The Constitution of The Reformed Church in America (Article 9, Section 4) states that the "Sacrament of Baptism shall be administered if possible at a time and place of public worship. The Office for the Administration of the Sacrament of Baptism must be read." Except for good reasons, Baptism shall be administered in the church. Parents or guardians must be present to assume the vows. The Church prohibits the practice of others assuming the vows for the parents or for the guardians.

The teaching of the Reformed Church concerning the nature of Baptism and the taking of the vows by the parents presupposes that at least one of them be a communicant member of the Christian Church (See Article 9, *The Constitution* R.C.A.). The mode of Baptism in The Reformed Church in America is generally that of sprinkling but immersion if desired is valid and proper.

The use of the prayers set forth in this form is not to be regarded as obligatory. As one of the Sacraments, Baptism should be administered after the service of the Word. See the outline for the proper sequence.

—The Constitution of
The Reformed Church in America

Seventh-day Adventists

"Baptism is an ordinance of the Christian church, the proper form being immersion, and should follow repentance and forgiveness of sins. By its observation faith is shown in the death, burial, and resurrection of Christ."
(Romans 6:1-6; Acts 16:30-33)

Baptismal vows, listed below, are taken voluntarily by prospective members just before baptism:

1. I believe in God the Father, in His Son Jesus Christ, and in the Holy Spirit.

2. I accept the death of Jesus Christ on Calvary as an atoning sacrifice for my sins, and believe that through faith in His shed blood men are saved from sin and its penalty.

3. I renounce the world and its sinful ways, and have accepted Jesus Christ as my personal Saviour, and believe that God, for Christ's sake, has forgiven my sins and given me a new heart.

4. I accept by faith the righteousness of Christ, recognizing Him as my Intercessor in the heavenly sanctuary, and claim His promise to strengthen me by His indwelling Spirit so that I may receive power to do His will.

5. I believe that the Bible is God's inspired Word, and that it constitutes the only rule of faith and practice for the Christian.

6. Loving the Lord with all my heart, it is my purpose, by the power of the indwelling Christ, to keep God's law of Ten Commandments, including the fourth, which requires the observance of the seventh day of the week as the Sabbath of the Lord.

7. I believe that my body is the temple of the Holy Spirit and that I am to honor God by caring for my body in abstaining from such things as alcoholic beverages, tobacco in all its forms, and from unclean foods.

8. I accept the doctrine of spiritual gifts, and believe that the Spirit of Prophecy is one of the identifying marks of the remnant church.

9. I believe in the soon coming of Jesus as the blessed hope, and it is my settled determination to prepare to meet Him in peace, as well as to help others to get ready for His glorious appearing.

10. I believe in church organization, and it is my purpose to support the church by my tithes and offerings, and by my personal effort and influence.

11. I accept the New Testament teaching of baptism by immersion, and desire to be so baptized as a public expression of my faith in Christ and in His forgiveness of my sins.

12. Knowing and understanding the fundamental Bible principles as taught by the Seventh-day Adventist

Church, it is my purpose by the grace of God to order my life in harmony with these principles.

13. I believe that the Seventh-day Adventist Church is the remnant church of Bible prophecy, into which people of every nation, race, class, and language are invited and accepted, and I desire membership in its fellowship.

—N.R. Dower, Secretary
General Conference of Seventh-day Adventists

UNITED METHODISTS
(The United Methodist Church)

Article XVI.—Of the Sacraments

Sacraments ordained of Christ are not only badges or tokens of Christian men's profession, but rather they are certain signs of grace, and God's good will toward us, by which he doth work invisibly in us, and doth not only quicken, but also strengthen and confirm, our faith in him.

There are two Sacraments ordained of Christ our Lord in the Gospel; that is to say, Baptism and the Supper of the Lord.

Those five commonly called sacraments, that is to say, confirmation, penance, orders, matrimony, and extreme unction, are not to be counted for Sacraments of the Gospel; being such as have partly grown out of the *corrupt* following of the apostles, and partly are states of life allowed in the Scriptures, but yet have not the like nature of Baptism and the Lord's Supper, because they have not any visible sign or ceremony ordained of God.

The Sacraments were not ordained of Christ to be gazed upon, or to be carried about; but that we should duly use them. And in such only as worthily receive the same, they have a wholesome effect or operation; but they that receive them unworthily, purchase to themselves condemnation, as St. Paul saith.

Article XVII.—Of Baptism

Baptism is not only a sign of profession and mark of difference whereby Christians are distinguished from others that are not baptized; but it is also a sign of regeneration or the new birth. The baptism of young children is to be retained in the church.

—The Book of Discipline of the United Methodist Church,
The United Methodist Publishing House

Article VI.—The Sacraments

We believe the sacraments, ordained by Christ, are symbols and pledges of the Christian's profession and of God's love toward us. They are means of grace by which God works invisibly in us, quickening, strengthening, and confirming our faith in him. Two sacraments are ordained by Christ our Lord, namely Baptism and the Lord's Supper.

We believe Baptism signifies entrance into the household of faith, and is a symbol of repentance and inner cleansing from sin, a representation of the new birth in Christ Jesus and a mark of Christian discipleship.

We believe children are under the atonement of Christ and as heirs of the Kingdom of God are acceptable subjects for Christian baptism. Children of believing parents through baptism become the special responsibility of the Church. They should be nurtured and led to personal acceptance of Christ, and by profession of faith confirm their baptism.

Evangelical United Brethren Church

The Order for the Administration of
the Sacrament of Baptism

† *Our ministers are enjoined diligently to teach the people committed to their pastoral care the meaning and purpose of the Baptism of children and to urge them to present their children for Baptism at an early age.*

† *When youth and adults present themselves for Baptism, the minister shall take due care that they have been instructed in the meaning of Christian Baptism.*

† *This Sacrament should be administered in the church in the presence of the people in a stated hour of worship. But at the minister's discretion this Sacrament may be administered at another time and place.*

† *This Sacrament may be administered by sprinkling, pouring, or immersion.*

† *The minister shall see that the names of all baptized children are properly recorded as preparatory members on the permanent records of the church, and in each instance he shall deliver to the parents or sponsors a certificate of Baptism.*

† *Children baptized in infancy shall be reported annually in the number of preparatory members until they shall have been received into full membership in the church or shall have attained their adulthood.*

—The Book of Worship for Church and Home
Board of Publication of The Methodist Church, Inc.

United Presbyterian Church in the U.S.A.

The Sacrament of Baptism

1. The Sacrament of Baptism is the Word made visible as ordained by Jesus Christ. It is a sign of God's love for us in Jesus Christ. It is a means by which men and women are called into the company of Christ's people. Christ was consecrated in his baptism as God's suffering servant, endured the servant's obedience to death, and was victorious over death in his resurrection. The baptism which the Lord has commanded his Church to observe is a consecration to the new life in Christ, which means faithful service and obedience and participation in the joy and victory of the resurrection. Baptism is both God's act and our response. In it God proclaims again and reassures us of his judging, forgiving, and redeeming love in Christ. By the work of his Spirit he marks us as his adopted children and enables us, God's people, in that same act to acknowledge the truth and power of the gospel, to accept God's forgiveness through repentance, to affirm our new identity as members of Christ's body, and to engage ourselves to be the Lord's in his ministry to all people.

Baptism is an act of the whole Church. It is a sign of entrance into the Church. It should, therefore, be regularly administered in the presence of the worshiping congregation. . .

Baptism marks a new beginning of participation in Christ's ministry for all people. This participation is an ever-expanding process and is not completed in the moment of baptism. The act of baptism sets us on a journey which lasts the whole course of our lives. As the baptism of Jesus anticipated the whole course of his obedience, so the meaning of our baptism becomes apparent only through the subsequent course of our lives as we practice what it means to be the Lord's in changing situations and in new relationships. . .

Baptism sets forth the grace of God in Jesus Christ and affirms that believers and their children are heirs of the covenant of grace. As the mode of entrance into the body of Christ, this sacrament need be administered only once to each person.

2. In the case of children of believers, sessions and ministers shall counsel parents that they have the responsibility of either presenting their children for baptism as infants or nurturing the children toward baptism upon their public profession of faith.

If they decide for baptism of an infant, the parents or the one(s) rightly exercising parental authority of the child promise to bring the child up to love God and serve him, and the members of the congregation likewise promise to surround the child with their concern and love in Christ, that the child may continue in the fellowship of the Church, confess Jesus Christ as Savior and Lord, and live in his eternal Kingdom.

At the time of baptism the child shall be recorded as a baptized member of the Church, and shall be numbered among those for whom the session has responsibility. The session shall offer continuing counsel, encouragement, and aid to the families of baptized children as they interpret the meaning of the Lord's Supper to their children. The session may authorize the families under its care to permit their baptized children to participate in the Lord's Supper with the congregation.

3. When persons baptized as infants reach an age when they are ready to participate more deliberately in the total life of the church, the session should invite, encourage, and help them prepare themselves for this greater responsibility. This preparation ought to include suitable instruction in the faith, worship, and mission of the church. The new role for which they are being prepared is that of participation in the governing and decision-making life of the congregation regarding its missions. Because the church ought to make decisions on the basis of its faith, a personal public profession of faith is a necessary part of entrance into governing responsibility. After appropriate examination, the session will admit these persons into their new role and provide for a service of commissioning.

The commissioning of baptized members is the public service before the congregation recognizing the admission of persons who were baptized as infants into voting rights in the congregation based on demonstration of sound knowledge of the faith, constitutional standards of the Church, and readiness to take responsibility for the tasks of ministry. It is an act whereby the Church recognizes the personal encounter with Jesus Christ as Lord and Savior of those who were baptized in infancy, and now desire to profess publicly their faith in him.

—*Book of Order*, "Directory for the Worship of God," United Presbyterian Church in the U.S.A.

JOHN'S BAPTISM OF REPENTANCE

Setting and Audience

Matt. 3:5. Then went out to him Jerusalem, and all Judaea, and all the region round about Jordan. 6. And were baptized of him in Jordan, confessing their sins. 7. But when he saw many of the Pharisees and Sadducees come to his baptism, he said unto them, O generation of vipers, who hath warned you to flee from the wrath to come? 8. Bring forth therefore fruits meet for repentance: 11. I indeed baptize you with water unto repentance: but he that cometh after me is mightier than I, whose shoes I am not worthy to bear: he shall baptize you with the Holy Ghost, and *with* fire.

John's Baptism of Jesus

Matt. 3:13. Then cometh Jesus from Galilee to Jordan unto John, to be baptized of him. 14. But John forbad him, saying, I have need to be baptized of thee, and comest thou to me? 15. And Jesus answering said unto him, Suffer *it to be so* now: for thus it becometh us to fulfil all righteousness. Then suffered him. 16. And Jesus, when he was baptized, went up straightway out of the water: and, low, the heavens were opened unto him, and he saw the Spirit of God descending like a dove, and lighting upon him (Mark 1:8-10; Luke 3:7,8; John 10:40).

Explanation of John's Baptism

Mark 1:4. John did baptize in the wilderness, and preach the baptism of repentance for the remission of sins. 5. And there went out unto him all the land of Judaea, and they of Jerusalem, and were all baptized of him in the river of Jordan, confessing their sins. Luke 3:12. Then came also publicans to be baptized, and said unto him, Master, what shall we do? 21. When all the people were baptized, it came to pass, that Jesus also being baptized, and praying, the heaven was opened.

Luke 7:29. All the people that heard *him,* and the publicans, justified God, being baptized with the baptism of John. 30. But the Pharisees and lawyers rejected the counsel of God against themselves, being not baptized of him.

John 1:25. And they asked him, and said unto him, Why baptizest thou then, if thou be not that Christ, nor Elias, neither that prophet? 26. John answered them, saying, I baptize with water: but there standeth one among you, whom ye know not; 28. These things were done in Bethabara beyond Jordan, where John was baptizing. 31. I knew him not: but that he should be made manifest to Israel, therefore am I come baptizing with water. 33. He that sent me to baptize with water, the same said unto me, Upon whom thou shalt see the Spirit descending, and remaining on him, the same is he which baptizeth with the Holy Ghost.

John 3:23. And John also was baptizing in Aenon, near to Salim, because there was much water there: and they came, and were baptized.

Jesus' Evaluation of John's Baptism

Matt. 21:25. The baptism of John, whence was it? from heaven, or of men? Mark 11:30; Luke 20:4.

Acts 1:5. John truly baptized with water; but ye shall be baptized with the Holy Ghost not many days hence. 22. Beginning from the baptism of John, unto that same day that he was taken up from us, must one be ordained to be a witness with us of his resurrection.

Peter's Acknowledgement of John's Baptism

Acts 10:37. That word, *I say,* ye know, which was published throughout all Judaea, and began from Galilee, after the baptism which John preached;

Acts 11:16. Then remembered I the word of the Lord, how that he said, John indeed baptized with water; but ye shall be baptized with the Holy Ghost.

Paul's Acknowledgement of John's Baptism

Acts 18:25. This man was instructed in the way of the Lord; and being fervent in the spirit, he spake and taught diligently the things of the Lord, knowing only the baptism of John.

Acts 19:3. And he said unto them, Unto what then were ye baptized? And they said, Unto John's baptism. 4. Then said Paul, John verily baptized with the baptism of repentance, saying unto the people, that they should believe on him which should come after him, that is, on Christ Jesus.

CHRISTIAN BAPTISM

Jesus' Statements

Matt. 28:19. Go ye therefore, and teach all nations, baptizing them in the name of the Father, and of the Son, and of the Holy Ghost.

Mark 16:16. He that believeth and is baptized shall be saved.

John 3:5. Jesus answered, Verily, verily, I say unto thee, Except a man be born of water and *of* the Spirit, he cannot enter into the kingdom of God. 22. After these things came Jesus and his disciples into the land of Judaea; and there he tarried with them, and baptized.

John 4:1. The Lord knew how the Pharisees had heard that Jesus made and baptized more disciples than John. 2. (Though Jesus himself baptized not, but his disciples,)

Acts 1:5. John truly baptized with water; but ye shall be baptized with the Holy Ghost not many days hence. 22. Beginning from the baptism of John, unto that same day that he was taken up from us, must one be ordained to be a witness with us of his resurrection.

Peter at Pentecost

Acts 2:38. Peter said unto them, Repent, and be baptized every one of you in the name of Jesus Christ for the remission of sins, and ye shall receive the gift of the Holy Ghost. 41. Then they that gladly received his word were baptized: and the same day there were added *unto them* about three thousand souls.

Philip Baptizes

Acts 8:12. When they believed Philip preaching the things concerning the kingdom of God, and the name of Jesus Christ, they were baptized, both men and women. 13. Then Simon himself believed also: and when he was baptized, he continued with Philip, *v.* 16.

36. And as they went on *their* way, they came unto a certain water: and the eunuch said, See, *here is* water; what doth hinder me to be baptized? [1]37. Philip said, If thou believest with all thine heart, thou mayest. And he answered and said, I believe that Jesus Christ is the Son of God. 38. And he commanded the chariot to stand still: and they went down both into the water, both Philip and the eunuch; and he baptized him.

[[1]Omitted in R.V.]

Saul's (Paul) Baptism

Acts 9:18. And immediately there fell from his eyes as it had been scales: and he received sight forthwith, and arose, and was baptized.

Acts 22:16. And now why tarriest thou? arise, and be baptized, and wash away thy sins, calling on the name of the Lord.

Peter at House of Cornelius

Acts 10:46. Then answered Peter, 47. Can any man forbid water, that these should not be baptized, which have received the Holy Ghost as well as we? 48. And he commanded them to be baptized in the name of the Lord.

Lydia Baptized

Acts 16:14. And a certain woman named Lydia, a seller of purple, of the city of Thyatire, which worshipped God, heard us: whose heart the Lord opened, that she attended unto the things which were spoken of Paul. 15. And when she was baptized, and her household, she besought *us*, saying, If ye have judged me to be faithful to the Lord, come into my house, and abide *there*.

Paul Baptizes Philippian Jailer & Family

Acts 16:33. He took them the same hour of the night, and washed *their* stripes; and was baptized, he and all his, straightway.

Corinthians Baptized

Acts 18:8. Many of the Corinthians hearing believed, and were baptized.

Ephesians Baptized

Acts 18:25. This man was instructed in the way of the Lord; and being fervent in the spirit, he spake and taught diligently the things of the Lord, knowing only the baptism of John.

Acts 19:4. Then said Paul, John verily baptized with the baptism of repentance, saying unto the people, that they should believe on him which should come after him, that is, on Christ Jesus. 5. When they heard *this*, they were baptized in the name of the Lord Jesus.

Paul on Baptism

Rom. 6:3. Know ye not, that so many of us as were baptized into Jesus Christ were baptized into his death? 4. Therefore we are buried with him by baptism into death: that like as Christ was raised up from the dead by the glory of the Father, even so we also should walk in newness of life.

I Cor. 1:13. Were ye baptized in the name of Paul? 14. I thank God that I baptized none of you, but Crispus and Gaius; 15. Lest any should say that I had baptized in mine own name. 16. And I baptized also the household of Stephanas: besides, I know not whether I baptized any other. 17. For Christ sent me not to baptize, but to preach the gospel:

I Cor. 10:1. Moreover, brethren, I would not that ye should be ignorant, how that all our fathers were under the cloud, and all passed through the sea; 2. And were all baptized unto Moses in the cloud and in the sea;

I Cor. 12:13. By one Spirit are we all baptized into one body, whether *we be* Jews or Gentiles, whether *we be* bond or free; and have been all made to drink into one Spirit.

I Cor. 15:29. What shall they do which are baptized for the dead, if the dead rise not at all? why are they then baptized for the dead?

Gal. 3:27. As many of you as have been baptized into Christ have put on Christ.

Eph. 4:5. One Lord, one faith, one baptism.

Eph. 5:26. That he might sanctify and cleanse it with the washing of water by the word.

Col. 2:12. Buried with him in baptism, wherein also ye are risen with *him* through the faith of the operation of God, who hath raised him from the dead.

103

Baptism in the Book of Hebrews

Heb. 6:2. Of the doctrine of baptisms, and of laying on of hands, and of resurrection of the dead, and of eternal judgment.

Peter on Baptism

I Pet. 3:18. Christ also hath once suffered for sins, the just for the unjust, that he might bring us to God, being put to death in the flesh, but quickened by the Spirit: 21. The like figure whereunto *even* baptism doth also now save us (not the putting away of the filth of the flesh, but the answer of a good conscience toward God,) by the resurrection of Jesus Christ.